Stepping

Olive Roberts

Stepping Stones.

Copyright © 2021 by Olive Roberts.

First edition, June 2021

DEDICATION

To Ron, my husband and best friend. Together we had a life of adventures. I miss those – and you – every day. Also, to all my grandchildren, Helen, Andrew, Megan, Philip, Catherine, Maiya and Luke, and to my great-grandchildren, PollyAnna, Alex, Alfie and Alana – and to all my future descendants whom I may never get to know but who are in my thoughts!

ACKNOWLEDGEMENTS

There are quite a few people I'd like to thank for making this book possible.

Firstly, my son Nigel, who has always had great faith in me, and is still making me perform miracles in my 90s. I hope I've lived up to his expectations.

I'd also like to thank my son Colin for all the photos he found, and for providing some family history. All my family have been supportive about this book, especially my grandchildren with their constant cries of 'Go on, grandma, you can do it!'

Thanks goes to Tom Henry. He sat for hours with me, dragging out memories I'd forgotten and then making all of it come to life. Without his help none of this would've happened.

I must not forget Keith Ougden for his expert proofreading, and particularly his assistance in the 'Cyprus' passages. Our lifetimes had many similarities and he's been a great help.

Last, but not least, my daughter-in-law Bella, who kept my spirits up during the first lockdown, making sure I had plenty to eat and never failing to turn up with a glass of wine, especially on my 92nd birthday. She came every week, and has been a guiding light when I felt like giving it all up.

CONTENTS

AUTHOR'S NOTE ABOUT PRE-DECIMAL CURRENCY AND AVERAGE EARNINGS

At various points in the book, mention is made of monetary amounts in terms that may be unfamiliar to younger readers. Terms such as "7 and 6", "thirty bob" and so on. This note explains what it all means.

For over 1,000 years, the pound had been divided into 20 shillings, and each shilling was made up of 12 pennies. So, there were 240 pennies in a pound.

On Sunday, 14th February 1971, that changed, and from then on the currency used in the UK became decimal-based.

On that day, something that cost £1 on 13th still cost £1 on 14th – so there was no change in the buying power of the pound, it was just divided in a different way.

The old currency had several coins, and quite a few had commonly used nicknames, as follows:

Farthing – 4 farthings to a penny (discontinued 1961)

Halfpenny (always pronounced "hape-knee", and written "ha'penny") – 2 to a penny (discontinued 1969)

Penny – 240 to a pound, 12 to a shilling. There wasn't a 2 penny coin, but 2 pennies were 2 pence, often pronounced "tuppence". (Mary Poppins: "Feed the birds, tuppence a bag…")

Threepenny piece – never pronounced "three-pence", but "threppence", or "throopence". Often the coin was known as a "threppenny bit" (or "throopenny bit")

The above coins were known collectively as "coppers", because of their colour. Someone short of money might ask to borrow "a few coppers".

Now we come to the "silver" coins, because of their colour (not because they were silver)

Sixpenny piece – worth six pence, 2 to a shilling. Sometimes known as a "sixpenny bit" and often known as "a tanner".

Shilling – 20 to a pound, worth 12 pence. This was very commonly known as a "bob", whether one or more than one. So something that cost 2 shillings would cost "two bob" (not two bobs). Note that there were 20 shillings to the pound. In the decimal currency a shilling is exactly the same fraction of a pound as a 5-pence coin today.

Florin – worth 2 shillings (or 2 bob). Exactly the same as the 10-pence coin today. Sometimes called a "two bob bit".

Half-a-crown – worth 2 shillings and sixpence – $2^{1/2}$ shillings. Often this was known as "half a dollar", because at one time 1 US Dollar was worth just 5 shillings (4 dollars to the pound!)

The notes were £1 ("a quid"), £5 ("5 quid", or "a fiver"), £10 ("a tenner")…

There was also a strange term "a guinea". This was 21 shillings, or £1 and 1 shilling (£1.05 today) Many businesses worked using "guineas", for example the art world, horse-racing. Even today, the term is used in horse-racing circles.

So how were amounts written? Well, one pound, seven shillings and eleven pence would be written as "£1-7-11", or "£1/7/11" or "£1-7s-11d". Note the "d" for pence. This comes from the Roman word "denarius". And you'd say "One pound, seven shillings and eleven pence", or, more often, "one pound, seven and eleven". To write just shillings and pence, seven shillings and six pence would be written "7/6" ("seven and six"). A flat seven shillings would be "7/-"

To put some of the monetary amounts used in the book in context, the average weekly wage for an agricultural worker has been (reference wirksworth.org)

1930: £1-11s (£1.55)
1935: £1-12s (£1.60)
1940: £2-8s (£2.40)
1945: £3-12s (£3.60)

1950: £4-19s (£4.95)
1955: £6-12s (£6.60)
1960: £7-18s (£7.90)
1965: £10-8s (£10.40)
1970: £13-3s (£13.15)
1975: £28.50
1980: £58.00. For all manual workers, £107.

From 1980 the figures shown are for all manual workers (reference UK Office for National Statistics)

1985: £159
1990: £232
1995: £288

From 2000 the figures are shown as overall average wage (reference tradingeconomics.com)

2000: £300
2005: £375
2010: £440
2015: £490
2020: £495

I once had a sweet little doll, dears,
The prettiest doll in the world;
Her cheeks were so red and so white; dears,
And her hair was so charmingly curled.
But I lost my poor little doll, dears,
As I played in the heath one day;
And I cried for her more than a week, dears;
But I never could find where she lay.

I found my poor little doll, dears,
As I played in the heath one day:
Folks say she is terrible changed, dears,
For her paint is all washed away,
And her arm trodden off by the cows, dears,
And her hair not the least bit curled:
Yet for old sakes' sake she is still, dears,
The prettiest doll in the world.

('My Little Doll', by Charles Kingsley, 1819-1875)

CHAPTER 1 – FIRST STEPS

My father was very fond of poetry. He used to recite verse after verse of it, and I would sit there, listening carefully to the words. The 'Little Doll' is one I remember distinctly, which is remarkable when you think about it because he died in 1934, when I was just six years old. His name was Joseph George Armstrong (always known as 'Joe'), he was born in the Northumberland market town of Morpeth and was the middle one of three children.

Back then, life could be short, hard and unpredictable. Children died young, and so did their parents. Early and sudden death, often from diseases long since eradicated, were regular occurrences. And when such things happened, those who'd gone were rarely talked about again. Certainly, that was the case in my family. Perhaps it was society's way of dealing with the awful events that marked everyone's lives.

My great-grandfather came from Cumbria and worked in a mill which made material from jute and flax which was tailored into prisoners' uniforms for those being transported to Australia. His son, also called Joseph, was an intelligent man (as was his son, my father), and at some stage around the turn of the 20th century he moved to Morpeth to work as a warder at St George's Hospital, built in 1859 and then known as the local 'lunatic asylum'. He also spent time as an insurance agent. I do not know how he met my grandmother Sarah (whose marriage to Joseph was her second) but it seemed her maiden name was Richardson and that she was originally from Portsmouth. Perhaps she had come up to the North East to be 'in service' at one of the big houses around Morpeth.

Anyway, they married and, as I've mentioned, had three children – Ellen, my dad (Joe) and Bob. Sadly, in 1900, Sarah died of TB and my grandfather made the decision to seek his fortune in America. Whether he achieved this or not we shall never know, because he never returned or sent for the children he'd left behind. The trio were farmed out to Joseph's two sisters, who raised them as best they could. Perhaps Joseph intended to bring the children over at some stage, but as he died in America the answer to this remains a mystery. I wonder now if we might be related to a couple of the famous American Armstrongs; Neil, the astronaut, or Lance, the cheating cyclist. Thinking about it, perhaps we'd rather not be related to him!

In 1914 the First World War broke out and all three siblings joined the war effort on the Western Front. Bob was with the Tyneside Scottish and was killed aged 19 on July 1, 1916 – the first day of the Somme. I've visited his grave out there, and just standing by it was an extraordinary feeling I'll not forget. Dad's sister Ellen was also out there as a nursing sister and, after Bob was killed, my father appealed to the authorities to release her from the Front, as her brother was dead and she had no parents. According to family legend, Ellen was killed by a shell which hit a casualty clearing station. As far as I know there is no official record of this, but it might be that she'd married and was serving under a different surname.

Dad enlisted a few days after war broke out and was in the

Cycling Corps, attached to the Northumberland Fusiliers. A 'cycling corps' sounds a strange organisation (and in fact, many years later, a junior Guards officer laughed heartily when I told him what my dad had done in the Great War, which I didn't take very kindly to) but at the start of the war it was considered that troops on bicycles could move much more rapidly than groups of infantrymen on foot. No doubt the cyclists got bogged down, like everyone else, in the mud of those terrible battlefields and it certainly wasn't a unit for the faint-hearted; my father was twice wounded in action before he was finally discharged from the army in January 1919.

During the war he attained the rank of Corporal, then Sergeant, but at some stage he was put on a charge for refusing to obey an order. He was due to be court-martialled but he pre-empted this by handing in his stripes and reverting to the rank of Private. I'm not sure what order he disobeyed but knowing my father it was probably a very stupid one. I expect by that stage in the war, he'd simply had enough of the whole business. Sadly, in September 1940 a German incendiary bomb which landed on the War Office Record Store in Arnside Street, London, destroyed about four million soldiers' records from the First World War, including my father's. What was left of his documents were charred and barely readable. This is very sad, as a full set of intact records would've given us so much more information on his war service.

One of the times my dad was wounded involved the use of poison gas, and when he came out of the army he made sure he didn't go back down the mine, where he'd been working before he enlisted. No doubt this was because his chest was bad, and so he drew out all his savings and trained to be a nurse at St George's Hospital in Morpeth, where his father had worked before him. It's possible that he had a bit of extra money in the form of pensions that were paid to him, being the next of kin of his deceased brother and sister. He did all the schooling and passed the exams that qualified him to be a nursing 'sister'. It was here that he met my mother, Mary Ellen Arthur, who was from the village of East Boldon and was working at the hospital as an assistant clerk. East Boldon is one of three close-knit communities (the other two being West Boldon and Boldon Colliery) that lay within County Durham and had close associations with the mining industry in that area.

My maternal grandfather, Peter Arthur, was born in 1866 in the seaside village of Cullercoats, which lies between Tynemouth and Whitley Bay, and was the son of a fisherman who owned and operated a herring-boat. Peter was the only son – the girls of the family were all employed cleaning the catch – and his father very much hoped Peter would follow the family tradition and become a fisherman himself. But there was one problem – young Peter was terrified of the sea! It was ironic, really, given that Peter's grandfather was a lifeboatman. He was attached to the station built in Cullercoats in the mid-Victorian era in response to a series of sinkings in the area, and it was funded by the Duke of Northumberland. Local men were paid a shilling every time they were called out, and as this was about a day's wages back then, unsurprisingly there was fierce competition among them to man the lifeboat when the call came.

The lifeboat was used in a famous rescue in 1861 when she was dragged overland several miles along the coast by six horses and many local men and women to rescue the crew of the brig 'Lovely Nelly'. The boat couldn't be launched at Cullercoats because of stormy weather.

No doubt Peter had been taken out in the herring-boat from an early age, but perhaps something had happened to put him right off the water. Anyway, so frightened was he of being pressured into something he hated that he ran away from home, never to return. I'm not sure what he did in the years leading up to his meeting with my grandmother but it's highly likely he was working in something farm-related because they first clapped eyes on one another at the 'hirings' at the Haymarket in Newcastle. These were regular events to which people in low-paid jobs such as farm work, labouring or 'in service' would go and wait until someone came along and offered them work.

My grandmother was at one of these gatherings when Peter Arthur came along. Margaret Elizabeth Heppenstall was born in Wallsend in 1869. Her mother, Margaret Heppenstall, had been married before under the name of Wilkinson, and strangely it was this name my grandmother used, rather than Heppenstall, when she married my grandfather. I've no idea why she did this, but I do know that if two of her many children were born in the same month, she'd change the date of their birthday to spread them out over the year!

Anyway, by all accounts, my grandmother's family were very poor. Her parents died young, and she, her sister Edith and her step-brothers went to live with an auntie who owned a shop. The boys went to work in the pits while my grandmother worked in the shop. As a child she never wore shoes and her family were so poverty-stricken that they were occasionally reduced to catching sparrows, killing them and toasting them in front of the fire. She once told me that one Christmas she was delivering some groceries to a big house. The lady who answered the door looked at this barefoot urchin in surprise and asked, "What did you get for Christmas?"

My grandmother looked back at her with equal surprise. "What's Christmas?" she replied.

I suspect my grandmother was working in service when she met my grandfather at the 'hirings', but she never admitted to this and claimed she was working on the land. Whatever the truth, she wasn't overly impressed by Peter's attentions and thought she'd got away from him when she was hired to work on a nearby farm. When she arrived, there he was, sat on one of the roofs, working!

He must have overheard the deal being struck between grandma and the farmer and decided to follow them. Eventually he must have persuaded her that he was a good catch because they went on to marry and have seven children – John William (known as 'John Willie'), Isabella ('Bella'), Tom, Joseph ('Joe'), Margaret Ella (known as 'Ella'), Edith May ('Eadie') and my mother, Mary Ellen (always known as 'Nell'). My grandfather couldn't read or write, signing the Register of Marriages with a cross where his name should have been.

For reasons that will become obvious, I'll leave my own impressions of my grandparents until later on in the story, along with what I know of the rest of their siblings. For now, let's turn back to my parents and the time I came along.

I was born one snowy morning in Morpeth. The date was March 27, 1928. By that stage my parents had been married for just under six years and had already suffered the loss of their first child, my brother Robert, otherwise known as 'Bobby' or 'Sonny'. Perhaps he was nicknamed the latter after the song made famous by Al Jolson, 'Sonny Boy', which was very well known at the time. I still have a photograph of Bobby, as my father was a keen amateur photographer, and in it he looks a bonny and robust little lad. Sadly for them, the poor child contracted meningitis and died at the age of just four in hospital in Newcastle. He was buried in the Armstrong family grave at St Mary's Church in Kirkhill, just outside Morpeth. My father was at the hospital when he died and in his grief-stricken state he left the hospital and walked home alone to Morpeth, a distance of 16 miles. I see him trudging along those dark and lonely roads, wrapped up in the kind of thoughts no parent ever wants to experience.

My mum and dad must have been devastated, but I don't remember them talking about Bobby much as I was growing up. I did hear stories about him from my grandparents, who had obviously loved him dearly and considered him an angel. My grandmother used to say, "Do you know, your brother Bobby could spell 'hippopotamus' and he was only four!" I do wonder whether, given this level of competition, I was an adequate replacement for Bobby, but anyway, I got on well with my parents, especially my father, with whom I spent a lot of time in my early years because he worked night shifts at the hospital and was often home for much of the day.

The house where I was born was in Hudson Place, which overlooked the River Wansbeck and was directly across from the stepping stones, which are still there today. The house, an old-fashioned back-to-back, is long gone, but I remember how the gardens of these houses stretched all the way down to the river. Dad had a lot of hobbies and was happy to share them with me. He enjoyed a game of bowls, and I would sit and watch him play while eating an ice-cream, or run after the bowled ball as it made its way to the jack. He was an excellent gardener and we had a wonderful garden full of roses. He kept his neighbours' gardens tidy, planting annuals so come summer the whole place was a riot of colour.

As I've mentioned, dad was a keen photographer and he would take snaps of family outings on the river, or picnics among the poppies in the cornfields. Film probably wasn't cheap then, and he used to snap me continually with his empty camera just to keep me quiet. One of my favourite pictures is of myself and my mother standing on the stepping stones. Just as he pressed the shutter my mother's hand has, for some reason, gone across my eyes. I can imagine him being furious at that! I know he was very proud when, as a tiny bairn, I won a 'bonny baby' competition organised by the 'Chronicle', the local newspaper. My cousin Elsie (my Auntie Bella and Uncle Peter's daughter who was only a teenager at the time) had come to Morpeth for a holiday and one day, as she was pushing me out in the pram, she saw a sign for the baby competition. Well, she entered me and I won! When dad was told she commented, "I'd have been annoyed if she hadn't." Miraculously, the news of my win still survives in a cutting from the newspaper, which my eldest son Colin found and has kept.

Having been in the army, dad was a patriot and he was involved in the formation of the local branch of the British Legion. Yet he was also very sympathetic towards the struggles of the working man – and at that time there was real struggle, especially in the North East. From what I gather he marched in sympathy with the miners at the time of the General Strike in 1926.

My mum also knew what hardship was. She was a clever girl, loved sewing and had an idea to be a tailoress. But grandma wouldn't hear of that and told her she'd be working on the land, just like everyone else. It was said that when my mother passed some school exams she came to the attention of her teacher, who asked my grandma to keep her in school because she could probably pass even more of them. Grandma refused, and so at a young age mum was sent away on a milk cart to take a place 'in service' and after lasting one day she hated it so much that she came straight back. I can imagine that didn't go down too well with my grandmother. Then mum went to Newcastle and during World War One spent some time sewing aeroplane wings in one of the local factories, most likely Armstrong-Whitworth's at Dukes Moor. Following that she came home to East Bolden and lived with my grandmother. This wasn't easy, because grandmother had suffered the loss of two sons, John Willie and Joe. John Willie joined up early and was in one of the Guards units. His job was looking after the horses which pulled the guns (he was an excellent horseman) and, just as in the 'War Horse' film, he had to take one of the horses from the farm he was working on over to France. At some stage he was badly injured, which left him blind, and he spent the rest of his short life in a convalescent home for wounded soldiers in Penshaw, where he eventually died.

Grandmother's troubles didn't end there. During the war another son, Tom, went missing presumed killed in Mesopotamia and although he was eventually found, suffering from terrible malaria, the stress of that must have taken its toll. But perhaps the hardest thing for grandma to bear was the loss of her son Joe, who was killed in 1918. With John Willie away it was down to Joe to run the farm and when he was conscripted grandma attended a court hearing in South Shields, begging the judge to spare him because John Willie was badly injured and Tom was still missing. The judge refused, saying, "My son had to go, and so does yours." Then Joe was killed just before the end of the war and my grandmother placed the whole house into mourning for a long time. This must have been miserable for the young girls growing up there. They weren't allowed any pleasures and if they managed to obtain any nice clothes they had to hide them away from the house and sneak out to get changed. Grandma had a pair of binoculars to spy on her girls, as she probably suspected what was going on.

So it isn't surprising that my parents liked their little luxuries in life. They weren't exactly well-off but they weren't doing badly when they eventually moved out of the back-to-back and went to live in a new council estate on the High Church estate in Morpeth. This would have been a real achievement for a couple like them. Now, they had everything they wanted (within reason) and seemingly they were happy with life.

Mum caught the 'health and fitness' bug which was going in the early 1930s and would wear a vest and shorts to take part in mass exercise classes. She was a real advocate of the benefits of fresh air, and when I was new-born I was placed in the pram and wheeled outside. My grandmother, who told me this story much later on, was horrified to find six inches of snow on my pram when she visited me just a few hours after my birth! My mum was also interested in fortune-telling and would go regularly, accompanied by me, to see what the future held for her. She would also become very annoyed at the way the cattle drovers beat their animals as they herded them to market in Morpeth, and she would stand there shouting at them as they passed by. I also remember going to the pictures with my parents and seeing, I think, Al Jolson in 'The Jazz Singer'. Maybe that's where I first heard the 'Sonny Boy' song that would've so resonated with my parents.

Unfortunately, the injuries my father sustained on the Western Front were to catch up with him, particularly the gassing. His chest was never the same after that and when I was about four years old he contracted TB. This is a nasty disease at the best of times, but when your chest is weakened there is very little hope. And so it proved for my father. After a year or so in a sanatorium there was nothing more that could be done for him and he was brought home to die. He was placed in my bed, while I shared with my mother, and I seem to remember a group of men standing at the foot of my bed. It was the occasion of the local annual fete and I was due to run in one of the children's races, which I stood a very good chance of winning. Unfortunately I had measles at the time and couldn't run that day. The men visiting my father must've felt sorry for me, and one of them reached into his pocket and gave me sixpence.

"Here, hinny," he said, "have this. You'da won, nae bother, if you'd been there."

They stood there, with heads bowed and their caps in their hands. Now I realise they must have been paying their respects to my dying father.

He passed away in 1934, leaving just my mother and me. I didn't attend his funeral at St Mary's Church – children rarely, if ever, went to funerals then. Instead, I think I spent the day with Mrs Dowie, whose husband was mayor of Morpeth and a friend of my father. I seem to recall her hiding thimbles under cushions to keep me entertained. Their house was opposite the church and so I expect it was a convenient place to leave me while the sad event took place across the road.

I don't know what happened in the aftermath, but I think we can be quite sure there was no life insurance pay-out or pension pot for my mother to rely upon. As far as I know she sold what possessions she had, and we moved to East Bolden and into my grandparents' house at 18, Front Street. Now, at the very least this would be a squeeze because this was a house with only two rooms; a large-ish kitchen-cum-living room and a tiny bedroom occupied by grandma and grandpa. I had already started school in Morpeth and now would have to swap to the local school in East Boldon. I didn't know it, of course, but this was to be the first of many moves during my schooldays.

The cottage was by the side of the main road through the village that linked Newcastle and Sunderland. Obviously, there was nowhere near the amount of traffic on the roads that there is today, so it was a relatively safe place to play. At the back of the house there was a small yard which was shared by another family and us. Luckily I had several aunts and lots of cousins dotted around the village, including Auntie Bella next door, so I was never short of company.

The lack of space in the house meant that my mother needed to find a live-in position somewhere else, and fortunately she secured a job in Newcastle as a housekeeper to a man named Charlie Crofton. I would be left with my grandparents during the week while mum earned money for us, and I didn't mind this at all. Apart from insisting I was clean when I went to bed, my grandmother allowed me such freedom as children today can only imagine. I particularly enjoyed sleeping in what we knew as the 'desk bed' in the living room; the bed was folded away and kept in a cupboard in the kitchen during the day.

As I nodded off to sleep, life went on around me. I used to lie very still and listen to all the stories and gossip swapped between my grandmother and her daughters. These are stories that I remember to this day, and quite a few are included in this book. Grandma didn't have electricity – she was far too Victorian for that – so I would settle down to the hiss of the gaslight, which would be dimmed by one of the aunties pulling a chain fitted to the mantle. Once they'd decided I was asleep they'd move next door to Auntie Bella's house, joined to grandma's house by a passageway, so the storytelling could continue without disturbing me.

But I wasn't always asleep when they left, and sometimes I'd lie awake and watch the lights of passing buses and cars flash around the room, lighting up grandma's pictures one by one. These were extreme examples of Victorian melodrama – one was called 'The Christian Martyrs' Last Prayer' and depicted weeping men and women tied up with ropes to rings on a wall, with howling and hungry lions trying to get to them. Another was 'The Wreck of the Hesperus', a famous painting that shows a little child tied to the mast of this ship as it sinks in heavy seas. Apparently it was a favourite of Queen Victoria but it did nothing for me – in fact, it haunted me for years, long after it was relegated to the lavatory in the back yard!

Despite the upheaval I quickly settled down at school and made lots of friends. I was always excited when weekends arrived, so that I could see my mum and spend the pocket money in the local sweetie shop. This situation carried on for some while until one Friday, when mum arrived home with news that would again see us packing our bags and moving on.

CHAPTER 2 – AN ORPHAN IS RESCUED

Mum was an elegant lady, good looking, and although widowed, still relatively young. The man she worked for, Charlie Crofton, was a widower with two children to look after – Joyce and Alan. Charlie Crofton had an elevated position as the Chief Sorting Officer in the General Post Office in Newcastle, and was on his way to taking the top job there. The inevitable happened, and quite soon mum was destined to be the next Mrs Crofton.

I was seven when this news was broken to me one Friday night when mum returned home to grandma's. No doubt I was the last to know. I certainly wasn't consulted about my feelings – in those days, the opinions of children were irrelevant. You did what you were told and that was that.

I missed my dad terribly. I missed the fun we'd had together; the photos he took of me with his camera and the way he poured sweet, sticky red syrup (which he called 'monkey's blood') all over the top of the ice-cream he'd bought me. I hoped that the new man in my mother's life would be as nice as the last one. For the time being, and until they were married, I was to call him 'Uncle

Charlie', and after the wedding I would be attending a new school close to the new house they were to have built that would accommodate us all.

Today, such sudden changes in the life of a small child would no doubt be managed very carefully, and given time for adjustment. Back then, things seemed to happen rather quickly, with not much consideration given to children's feelings. You just 'got on with it' and made the best from the situation.

Eventually I was taken to meet my new family, who were living in Fenham, a smart suburb of Newcastle to the west of the city. Alan and Joyce greeted me and, because this was December, were proud to show me the Christmas tree that had just been put up in their house. I was very impressed; grandma never wanted one, and even if she had there would have been precious little space to accommodate it. That said, she and granddad did put up a 'mistletoe bough' every Christmas that was fashioned from the metal hoops that strengthened wooden beer barrels and decorated with mistletoe and greenery found locally.

I was also impressed by the fact that Joyce had her own bedroom, which I was allowed to sleep in, and eventually I was spending most weekends with the Croftons. Joyce was a few years older than me and Alan a few years younger, but we got along well enough and I don't remember any rivalry between us. I cannot recall if I attended my mother's wedding. I don't think I did; given that it was a second marriage for both of them, perhaps it was a low-key affair at a register office. Following the wedding, the new house in Denton Burn, again to the west of Newcastle, was ready for us to occupy and the five of us moved in. I started my new school, Wickham View (which was also newly built, in the art deco style). However, my mum still had a fixation with the health benefits of the great outdoors and quite soon I swapped Wickham View for Pendower Open-Air School, opened in 1925 and located in a Victorian mansion in Benwell, Newcastle. The idea was that children attending the school would benefit from as much exposure to the elements as possible and this really caught my mum's imagination. I enjoyed it there and was happy playing and learning outside.

So we settled into life in Denton Burn quite well. It was certainly very different from grandma's house in East Boldon. We were quite well off and mum seemed very happy making lots of well-to-do friends. They all called her 'Mrs Crofton', which sounded very posh to me. We played out in the street and went on visits to parks, museums, galleries, castles and the like. When the fair came to the Town Moor, a huge open area in Newcastle, we all went together and had a super time winning coconuts on the shies. After the trauma of losing my dad it seemed that life was good again, and although I still felt awkward calling Charlie Crofton 'Dad' (secretly I still thought of him as 'Uncle Charlie') he was a nice man who obviously cared a lot about my mum and me.

At some stage in 1936 mum announced that she was pregnant. I'm not too sure if I ever knew that she was, but I do remember a row between mum and Uncle Charlie about some tests she was required to take. She could be very stubborn, and on this occasion was refusing to go because she felt perfectly well. Her stubbornness might have been her undoing because soon afterwards she had a huge haemorrhage and although she managed to give birth, tragically she died in the process. I'm not sure she knew she was carrying twins…

The events of that day are hazy. I arrived home from school to a scene of chaos, grief and bloodshed. The babies, who had both survived, were brought downstairs in a clothes basket. No one told me anything, but it was obvious something terrible had happened. I was eight years old, and no doubt in a state of numbed shock about what had just happened. For the second time, I did not attend the funeral of my parent, and to all intents and purposes, I was now an orphan.

The immediate problem in the aftermath of my mother's death was what to do with the new babies, now named Edith and June, who of course were my step-sisters. In those days, the idea of a widowed man caring for new babies alone would have perhaps been considered unfeasible, so the two were taken away to a nursing home, where they were eventually put up for adoption. Aunt Eadie, my mother's sister, decided to take on Edith, but the fate of June was to remain a mystery for many years.

Of course, now my mother was dead I didn't 'belong' to anyone, and certainly not to the Croftons. Uncle Charlie hadn't officially adopted me at the time of my mum's death, so I wasn't his responsibility. He probably had enough on his plate at the time. A short while after the funeral some friends of my mother arrived from Newcastle to see what was going on, and during the course of a conversation it emerged that Charlie Crofton had no idea what to do with me. This was relayed back to my grandparents in East Boldon and my granddad said to grandma, "Just go and get her."

So she put on her coat, caught the bus to Charlie Crofton's, and did just that. And I think this was the first time I found out what had happened to my mother. For the second time, my home was to be in that well-kept but nonetheless tiny house in East Boldon, and I would be there much longer than I, or anyone else, could've anticipated.

Having decided to take on baby Edith, Aunt Eadie instructed her husband, Uncle Billy, to begin the formal proceedings of adoption. Billy was an accountant at the Shire Hall in Newcastle and knew Charlie Crofton quite well. They spoke about the legalities and concluded that it would be a good month before the adoption went through. In the meantime, Aunt Eadie decided that she needed a holiday before she faced the pressures that the new arrival would bring, so she and her daughter Norrie rented a cottage in Scarborough and I was invited to go with them. We were there for a month and had a lovely time. I always got on well with my cousin Norrie; she was very tomboyish and although I had no idea at the time, later on it would become obvious she was gay.

Anyway, the month passed by and finally Aunt Eadie and Uncle Billy were ready to remove little Edith from the nursing home and make her their own. When they arrived, they were shocked by what they saw. Already small, Edith seemed under-nourished, couldn't breathe very well and wasn't in a particularly clean state. They insisted on a full medical examination of the child, and only when she was given a clean bill of health did they take her home to Durham. The other baby, June, had already gone, destination unknown. It seems incredible now that the authorities could allow twins to be separated so easily, but like many events I've mentioned, that's 'just how it was' back in the good old days!

I was a bright child and at eight years old I was fully aware that Edith was my relation; technically a half-sister but a sister all the same. I would tell people that I had a baby sister who lived in Durham, but possibly I mentioned this to the wrong person, because on my next visit to Aunt Eadie and Uncle Billy's I was summoned into Aunt Eadie's bedroom. She was ever so much 'the lady', and even had a gas fire in her boudoir – a luxury unknown to us in East Boldon.

"I understand you're telling everyone that baby Edith is your sister," she said as I stood in front of her.

I wasn't sure how to reply. "I can't remember if I did or not," I said, trying to fudge the truth.

Aunt Eadie stared at me disapprovingly. "Well," she said finally, "from now on Edith is your cousin, not your sister. You will refer to her as your cousin, never your sister. And you will not mention it to anyone. Do you understand?"

I nodded. Children then never took issue with the judgements of adults. I assume that Aunt Eadie never wanted Edith to know she was adopted and if she said Edith was my cousin then that's what she was, and the matter was closed. And in all the years that passed, until a terrible tragedy befell the family, I never did mention it. But more of this later.

In the meantime I returned to my old school in East Boldon and settled into life at grandma and granddad's. They were neither young nor well-off, and having sole responsibility for an eight-year-old couldn't have been easy. Granddad had been a farm worker all his life and was now living on his pension. Grandma was ten years his junior, but even so she was well into her sixties and must have had to rearrange her way of life to accommodate me. They must have done this with very little complaint because I was just happy to be back 'home' and into the arms of a 'normal' family – if there is such thing as a normal family, which I very much doubt! I suppose I was a very adaptable child, but it may be that very few references to my deceased parents meant that I didn't dwell on my status as an orphan. I lived a happy-go-lucky life, with not a care in the world.

I had a wild spirit that enjoyed tearing up and down the back alleys and lanes, paddling in brooks and playing with rubbish we found in farmyards and old abandoned buildings. My life in East Boldon was in sharp contrast to the life my cousin Norrie and her new sister Edith were living in Durham. We visited them quite regularly and I always enjoyed seeing them, but often I found the time we spent there quite boring, because the only area we were allowed to play in was the garden, riding round and round the flowerbeds on a tricycle or swinging endlessly on the garden swing. We played with dolls and teddies, and at the time I really envied Norrie for the toys she had. Now I see that my home life in East Boldon was much richer in spirit, if not in wealth.

I looked forward to the long summer holidays, and getting

together with the gang of kids to look for fun and adventure. Much of this was spent in and around the local hayfields. We would travel there on hay bogeys which were pulled by big shire horses. In any case, the local farmers didn't seem to mind us kids clambering aboard the flat-bedded bogey and travelling to the hayfields with our legs dangling over the side of the cart.

When we arrived at the hayfield we'd play in the stooks (the sheaves piled up prior to collection) while the farm labourers gathered up the hay. Sometimes we were told off if we got in the way; most times no one bothered us. Once the bogeys were piled high with hay we were allowed to climb up to the top of the stack, sometimes to a height of twenty feet or so, and enjoy (or endure!) the bumpy ride back to the farm in time for lunch. After that, and once the bogey was cleared, we'd hop on to it again and enjoy a long, golden afternoon in the hayfield. Imagine today's children being allowed to do this!

Then there were the trips to the seaside. Buses would take us to small seaside towns and villages like Seaburn, Whitburn, South Shields, Tynemouth and Whitley Bay. Summers along the North East coast could be cold and wet but when the sun was out there was no finer place to be. We didn't bother too much about the huge steel pipes that ran from the promenade across the beach and into the sea. We knew they were pumped full of raw sewage, but we ate our egg and tomato sandwiches while sitting on them and didn't worry at all about what was going on underneath. My gran would take her own bread and would cut it on her lap with a carving knife. I would hide my eyes and shout, "Grandma, you'll kill yourself!" She always brought her own butter, which she made at home with my assistance, and would give me the lion's share of it to build me up.

We ate a lot of dripping, which I enjoyed, and I loved it when gran mixed dripping and Bovril on to a slice of bread for me. She was a decent cook, apart from pastry which always seemed to be soggy, but she made sure I never went without anything and she could make a meal out of nothing. Mind you, she didn't teach me to cook because she'd have considered it a waste of food if I'd burned something. Living quite near the coast we had a lot of fish and I loved rollmop herrings, especially when they were cold.

When I was six, and living in East Boldon after my father's death, I joined the Brownies. And in various ways, I was involved in Brownies and Guiding for the next 40 years or so! When I moved away to live with the Croftons I took a break, but following my return to East Boldon after mum's death, I re-joined the local pack. The Brownie meetings were held in the village hall, which was next door to my grandmother's house. Mrs Brock, wife of the local butcher, was in charge of the pack. You would enrol by promising to do your duty to God and The King, and following this you were allowed to wear your brown-coloured uniform complete with tie, which was fastened with a reef knot at the back of the neck, and a badge depicting a little elf-like creature.

We were awarded badges for simple activities like making a cup of tea and elementary knitting. I learned how to make the tea, but Aunt Ella helped me knit a vest and gran assisted when it came to making a batch of scones. During the meetings a little carved wooden toadstool was brought out from a store cupboard and we would all dance around it, singing various songs. Because I was in the Fairy troop, my song was:

"I'm a fairy, bright and gay, helping others every day."

Members of the Gnome pack would sing:

"Here we see the little gnomes, helping mothers in their homes."

The Elves song went something like:

"Here you see the little elves, helping others, not themselves."

And as for the Pixies – I'm afraid I can't remember what they sang!

When I was 10, I 'flew up' from the Brownies into the Guides.

This process of moving on involved you sitting in a dark cupboard while other Brownies, Guides and Guide leaders sang scary songs to you. When it was deemed you were sufficiently terrified, the door was opened and you 'flew out' and jumped up from the Brownies to the Guides with a big leap.

The Guide Captain, a Mrs Brock, lived close to my gran's house and she was lovely. She was the churchwarden's adopted daughter. She'd take us tracking across the fields - we would lay tracks with bits of wood to show the way to go, and others followed us. She would also teach us games like 'Sleeping Princesses', where we'd take turns to creep across the village hall in the hope of not disturbing the 'Princesses' lying on the floor.

A semi-permanent fixture outside the village hall was my grandfather, who would sit on a bench with a few of his old cronies while they waited for the pub to open. My gran would look out of the window and remark, "Aye, the pub's open now – just look at them all going in."

Gran would give granddad an allowance of just half a crown each week, which had to cover his beer, baccy and mints. She was definitely the boss – if he wasn't on the bench he'd be sitting on a rocking chair in the living room, and I remember being told that one night he decided to put more coal on the fire while gran was out at her W.I. meeting. She was frugal, and had already banked the fire up, so she would have been most displeased to know he was putting extra fuel onto it. This particular evening he'd also decided to draw the settee up close to the fire and shortly before her return he decided to move it back to its original place, so she would suspect nothing. So he went round to Mrs Gibson, who lived next door. Lily, her daughter, answered.

"Lily, could you give us a hand, hinny?" he said. "She'll be back soon and I need to move the settee."

The young girl and the old man heaved the settee back into place and granddad was sure all was well. But grandma could feel how warm the room still was and no doubt granddad got an earful from her!

Generally, though, he enjoyed his life. He taught me how to dry dishes and cups because gran would ask me and I'd no idea. He was lovely to me, making me the best wooden tops in the street. These could be spun along the paving stones with the tiniest flick of a little whip, which he'd also make from a thin stick and a knotted piece of string. With this I could whip the top along and even lift it up and across the road, still spinning.

We regularly used the main road for our games. We'd all try to do handstands against various walls or we'd have mass skipping contests. The fruit shop sold sweeties, so we'd spend a lot of time with our noses pressed up against the shop window. We would also play a game called 'Jack Shine Maggie', in which we'd have to locate each other in the dark with the use of a torch. This was a lot of fun in the years leading up to 1939, but by the autumn of that year this game would be consigned to history, and we had no idea when we would be playing it again. War had been declared, the blackout was in force, and all our lives would change dramatically over the next five years.

Chapter 3 – Schooldays and Sirens

Although we'd all known that war was coming for a while, people chose not to think about it. Until September 3, 1939, my life was idyllic and even though I'd lost both parents I had a family all around to look after me.

By the time war broke out I was sharing a bed with my grandmother. Not an ideal situation, really, as she was a big woman who tossed, turned and snored at night, but I had grown too big for the desk bed. Also, there was now room next to my grandmother following the death of my grandfather a year previously.

As I've mentioned, he was an old man and had had a hard life. His passing was mourned, of course, because he had been popular around East Boldon, walking to the pub in his smart tweed suits, cap, gloves and shiny brogues. When he died of old age he was laid out in his bed as custom dictated so that friends and neighbours could pay their respects. I recall sneaking past the door and peeping through a gap to look at his body. On the evening after his funeral I was lying in that very bed with my grandmother next to me. Imagine that happening now! Of course, I thought nothing of it; there were no other bedrooms in the house so it was a natural move.

In the summer of 1939, the question came up of my secondary schooling. I was a bright girl and my grandmother knew that, by rights, I should attend a grammar school. However, she was far too poor to be able to afford that, so she started to apply for scholarships, which I would qualify for if I was able to pass the entrance exams. My teacher at the primary school in East Boldon, Miss Dury, had faith in my ability. She had kept a special eye on me since I was eight. At that stage she'd set the class an essay entitled 'My Mother'. There wasn't much to say about mine so I simply wrote, "My mother is dead." Then I started crying and couldn't stop. When Miss Dury saw what I'd written she said, "Oh Olive, don't be silly – your mother's not dead. She's just had a baby, that's all!" For some reason the very recent news about my mother hadn't reached her and when she learned the truth she was shocked. So I was fed tea and cakes and sent home for the rest of the day, and after that she looked out for me.

Miss Dury helped my grandmother to locate suitable scholarships, and one was found at a girls' grammar school in Washington. The exam was in two parts and I passed the first one easily, to the surprise of my grandma. The second part was to be held in Washington, so a friend and I took the bus there, on our own, and when we arrived, the school felt like another world – certainly like nowhere two girls from East Boldon had ever experienced. It seemed to be very big and posh and rule-bound. We ate our sandwiches in the playground and, perhaps overawed by the whole experience, somehow made ourselves late for the exam. Anyway, I never actually took this part and so the idea of going to school in Washington was over.

Miss Dury was surprised, and urged my grandma not to give up on me just yet. She felt I could've passed it, and suspected that somehow I'd just had an 'off-day'. She identified another school in Sunderland that was prepared to take bright but poor children and this time I knuckled down and passed the exam. The tuition would be free, but money would be needed for books, uniform, sports equipment and the rest. My grandma went into a panic. She only had a widow's pension and a small orphan's pension for me. There was another tiny amount of money from the War Office, resulting from her losses in the Great War, but really that was it.

She wrote to the British Legion, on the strength of my father's war service, and also to the Freemasons, as he had been a member of a Morpeth Lodge. They both offered some assistance but it wasn't financial, so I'm not really sure what kind of support was on the table from them. Anyway, suddenly all the worrying stopped, and before school started I was taken to Sunderland to be fitted out for the lovely royal blue and yellow uniform, complete with Panama hat for the summer and a woollen pull-on one for wintertime. I only learned many years later how grandma managed to buy all this. It appeared that she needed to know my father's service number, which was printed on his medals. For some reason these were still in the possession of Charlie Crofton, my mother's second husband, so grandma wrote to him and asked him for them, explaining why she needed them. When Mr Crofton heard, he agreed to pay for whatever I needed and would deposit three guineas a term into my grandmother's bank account for any expenses. So he did us a great favour – and so he should've done!

The day war broke out was a Sunday and I was either at church or going to church when Chamberlain made the broadcast. Although we expected it, when it came the news was shocking. Just after the announcement was made my Auntie Ella came running down the road, shouting at the top of her voice. "Where are my children?!" she screamed, "the bombs will be falling any minute!"

Of course, nothing happened for a long time but Aunt Ella's reaction was typical of the fear many people felt when they heard the news. And it was typical of Ella to react in this way. She was my grandma's youngest daughter and she was, as they say, a real character. She was married with a son and a daughter but she made sure she kept her good looks intact, for she was never averse to an admiring glance. She was one of these eternally youthful people who enjoy having a good time, and Uncle Albert, her husband, just had to go along with her lively spirit. She would come into my grandma's house, sit on the kitchen table ('on', not 'at') and swing her legs as she gossiped away. Because she was the baby of the family, she could get away with it.

Uncle Albert was a nice man. He worked for a big firm of road-menders and drove a steamroller. Like my dad, he'd been gassed in the First World War and was never in the best of health. When the Second World War broke out he volunteered to become an Air Raid Precautions Warden along with other village men, whom he looked up to and admired. Eventually he became confined to bed and I would run errands to the local library to get his favourite Western novels. I remember him telling me one day that the doctor was coming, and I felt sorry for him because he and Ella had no carpet on the floor. So I spoke to my cousin Elsie about it and she offered to remove the rug from her bedroom to lend them. We took it round and Uncle Albert was so grateful.

The rug was never mentioned again and some months later Uncle Albert died. After the funeral Elsie suggested we get the carpet back so we went round and Aunt Ella was out. We located it, rolled it up and took it back to Elsie's – and it still wasn't mentioned again!

Ella was a wild character, with her dark hair and green eyes, but I liked her immensely, even when she used to get me into trouble by claiming that I'd escorted her to various local dances that I'd not even been at because I was too young!

So the first day at my new school coincided with the first full day of World War Two. I went to Sunderland on the bus and once there I took a tram to Durham Road, where the school was located in various old buildings. I settled in quickly and particularly enjoyed English and poetry. I loved acting and was once picked to play Ariel in The Tempest. That evening I came home to East Boldon and proudly announced the news to those gathered in grandma's kitchen. There was no small amount of eye-rolling, then Elsie piped up, "I didn't know they picked fairy elephants for Shakespeare plays." Typical of that lot to put you down!

I quite liked the idea of swimming, as there was a pool at the school, but I was less than pleased when the French teacher (who was herself French) pushed me in, in an attempt to get me going. Before this incident I had admired the Mademoiselle, as we had to call her. She was young and pretty, and got us to learn and sing La Marseillaise, the French national anthem, which I can recall to this day:

Allons enfants de la Patrie
Le jour de gloire est arrivé
Contre nous de la tyrannie
L'étendard sanglant est levé

And so on! After the fall of France in May 1940 the Mademoiselle disappeared and there were rumours that she'd been parachuted into France to join the Resistance.

I regularly played shinty (a Scottish version of hockey) at school until the playing field was eventually turned over into allotments for the production of food. The swimming pool was drained and met the same fate. As the months went on, the war crept into all aspects of our lives. We were bombarded by lots of information about what to do if there was an air-raid, and ration books were issued by the Ministry of Food. One day we were all summoned to the village hall in East Boldon to collect our gas masks. I'll never forget the smell of rubber and the overwhelming feeling of claustrophobia when the appliance was placed over my face and the straps tightened. The whole thing was then tested by holding postcards over the breathing tube to see if it was air-tight, and it was a great relief to finally be able to pull the wretched thing off my head.

Cousin Elsie, who was now married with two children, was in an absolute panic about all of this. Her eldest daughter, Margaret, completely refused to have her 'Mickey Mouse mask' anywhere near her face while her youngest, Pat, was still a tiny baby and had to be placed in a tank-like box.

"We'll all end up being gassed," Elsie sobbed, tears streaming down her face, "because none of us will have time to put our masks on."

Meanwhile, grandma was making faces and pretending she was fainting at the thought of it all, only to get her hair caught in the webbing when the mask was pulled from her face. It was a good job gas was never used, as it would've been like something out of a Carry On film! Grandma was asked if she would head up a local unit of volunteers who would get to work extinguishing incendiary bombs should they land on the village. A group of official-looking men put this request to her while standing on her doorstep and she probably wasn't in a position to refuse. However, the tin hat she was issued was made into a lovely hanging basket, and the stirrup pump she would need to tackle whatever the Luftwaffe could throw at her became a very useful device for emptying the wash tub on washing day.

I also remember grandma showing me the first ration book she had. I looked at all the coupons and assumed that you gave these in at the butcher's and grocer's and received all your meat and veg for free. Grandma had to explain exactly what 'rationing' meant….

At school, the siren was regularly sounded for practice and every time we had to undergo the same drill, diving under our desks to wait for the all-clear. All the windows were done up with tape to stop them shattering in the event of bombs falling, and at home, we had to completely black out our cottage windows or dire consequences were threatened by the Wardens who patrolled the area. Grandma concocted a wonderful blackout device from a piece of paper that completely covered the window frame and had to be wedged into place every night. It was cumbersome but effective, especially when compared to other people's flimsy blackout curtains, and she persisted with it right to the end of the war, long after German aircraft had ceased to be a threat.

Having moved up to the Girl Guides, I was expected to do my bit for the war effort. We helped to collect silver paper and scrap metal to be turned into aeroplanes, tanks and Lord knows what, and we knitted for the troops. All I can say is that some very weird and wonderful scarves and balaclavas went out to the front line. We also collected money for men in POW camps; the money was sent to the Red Cross, who purchased everyday items to be sent off in their famous parcels. We took part in 'Wings For Victory' parades and concerts, helping to raise money for urgently needed fighter planes. At the age of 14 I joined the Junior Women's Air Corps and we did a big show at the Sunderland Empire, all of us very proud in our new blue uniforms. I recall us singing a song which went something like:

Flying high, flying high, we're over the moon today
Listen to the roaring, as we go soaring…

At the time, Sunderland was a huge shipbuilding town crucial to the war effort, and every time I went to and from school I noticed the shipyards almost permanently lit up with the flashes from welding guns as the workers rushed to make more and more warships. After the Blitz on London it was obvious that the

Germans would look to disrupt production wherever they could, and the shipyards of the North East were prime targets. It was only a matter of time before they would be attacked, and it wouldn't just be the shipyards that would suffer damage and destruction. A year or so into the war the decision was made to evacuate the whole school to the countryside near Durham. For whatever reason, grandma decided that I wouldn't be going with them – most likely it was the distance involved in getting to and from the school, and if the bombs did start falling, she wouldn't have wanted me stuck on the school bus.

Instead, she decided to enrol me into Thornhill Commercial College in Sunderland, which specialised in turning out girls ready to work in offices as shorthand typists. It was a far cry from my beloved poetry and Shakespeare, but at 12 or 13 years old I wasn't in a position to argue with grandma, who seemed to know best. So I went along dutifully, and met with the head of the college, the Reverend Hutler. There are no prizes for guessing what nickname the trainee typists gave him!

Rev Hutler taught shorthand and although he was a strange man in many ways, he certainly knew his stuff. He was a brilliant teacher and in no time at all I became very good at the Pitman's system of shorthand, and to this day I can still write it. We passed the shorthand exams in increments; 80 words per minute, then 100, 120 and finally 140 words per minute, writing down four minutes of speech then transcribing it perfectly. I mastered typing but it was a subject I tolerated rather than loved. Book-keeping I hated; I've never been great with figures.

Overall, though, I did very well at the Commercial College and by the age of 14 I was more than qualified to begin office work. Perhaps this is why Rev Hutler summoned me to his office one afternoon with a proposition.

"Miss Armstrong, do you think you'd be interested in a job?" he said. "I'm told there is an office vacancy at Books Fashions. I think it would be splendid work for a girl of your abilities."

Well, I was bowled over. A job! And in Books Fashions, which at the time was the most popular shop of its kind in the town. Even my grandma, whose interest in clothes didn't really extend beyond a black dress and a pinafore, would pop in there from time to time. It seemed very posh to me, and I could see myself walking through its doors every day and admiring all the lovely clothes on display.

I was very excited, but also cautious. In the back of my mind I knew that grandma wanted better things for me – which, in her mind, was probably a job in a solicitor's or a doctor's, leading to marriage with the said solicitor or doctor. If I told her about Rev Hutler's suggestion the reply would be a flat 'No'. So I did the next best thing, and didn't tell her at all.

In secret I went for the interview at the shop in Park Lane, and they seemed lovely, wanting me to start as soon as I could. So when the following Monday came I prepared for school as usual, knowing my grandma wouldn't suspect anything. Then I got the bus into town for my first full day at work. And I loved it. My tasks included dealing with the clothing coupons - first I'd count them, then weigh them as a cross-check that the count was more-or-less correct. Then I would take them to the post office where they'd be weighed again for verification. The people in the office were very nice to me, including old Mr Books, the Jewish owner of the shop, and on the third day he suggested I might like to spend some time in the hats department. So I went down and helped a lovely lady to steam-press the felt around various formers to shape the hats, then dress up the finished hats with bits of ribbons, net and flowers made from felt. I enjoyed it so much that I completely forgot to take my lunch hour, and as I went home on the bus I was thrilled to have such an interesting job.

Friday came, and I was given 15 shillings in wages for the week.

It seemed such a large amount of money then. However, I had something of a dilemma. The shop always closed on a Wednesday, which wasn't a problem because I was able to tell my grandma that I'd been at college. But it was open on Saturdays, and somehow I'd have to find an excuse to go into town every Saturday without fail. So I took the situation into my own hands, plucked up courage, and when I arrived home I placed the brown envelope on the kitchen table.

My grandma stared at it for a few seconds before speaking.

"What's this?" she said, eyeing it suspiciously.

"It's my wages," I replied, as sweetly as I could.

"I beg your pardon?"

"It's my wages," I repeated. "Fifteen shillings. I've been working. I've got a job."

"What job?" Now grandma's mood had really darkened.

I told her about Books and the coupons and the hats and the ribbons. And the nice staff, and how lovely old Mr Books was. But it cut no ice with the old lady.

"I'll give you 'job'!" she shouted. "I can't believe I'm hearing this! I've just been to the post office to draw out your orphan's 7 and 6. You'll have the police on me now!"

And with that, she chased me round the kitchen table and out into the yard. I was too quick for her, dodging the swipes from her open hand, but it was her words, not deeds, that really upset me. She swore that she would take me down to Books Fashions the following day, where I would collect my cards. "But I don't have any cards!" I protested.

"No cards!" she shouted. "What sort of a place is this?"

Anyway, she was as good as her word and the next day she escorted me into town and straight to the store. She knew old Mr Brooks and as soon as we arrived his face lit up.

"Oh, I didn't realise you were Olive's grandmother, Mrs Arthur," he said. "Such a lovely girl. We're so enjoying her working for us."

Red-faced, grandma explained that I'd taken the job behind her back, and that I would be leaving immediately. Mr Books pleaded with her to let me stay, citing my good work in the office and the hat department. She would hear none of it, claiming that she 'went down on bended knees' to pay for my education, and that as a result I would not be working in a clothes shop.

However, grandma didn't seem to be averse to me doing some kind of work, and so she arranged for me to have an interview with a legal firm called MacKenzie & Co. I was offered the position of junior clerk, on ten shillings a week (less than I was being paid at Books!) and longer hours. There wasn't much to be cheerful about but I'd sort of brought this on myself and just accepted it.

My work started when all the legal correspondence had been typed. I was given baskets of the stuff, which were typed in purple ink and had to be copied separately on a Roneo machine. This was loaded with a wet roll of thin tissue-like paper, known in the office as 'bumph'. I would feed the letters through the rollers which pressed the paper onto the bumph, making a copy from the purple-ink original. Can you imagine what these letters were like when I had finished with them?!

This wet roll of copy letters was guillotined off and, once dry, put into a folder ready to be filed and cross-matched with previous ones on the same subject. Then they had to be put into envelopes and sent off. I did my best with all this, but it often took me ages, and I would enlist the help of the cleaner to read out names and addresses while I typed the envelopes ready for posting.

It was quite a boring job, but I can't say I hated it because I liked the other people working there. Besides, a lot of my friends were junior clerks in the same area so we'd have great fun meeting each other during the morning, delivering letters that didn't need posting and scouring the local shops for anything that might not be 'on the ration'. No one in the office seemed to miss me, and I would take orders from the typists for Drene shampoo, lipsticks, combs, soap, hairgrips – in fact, anything that Woolworth's might have a stock of. These things were very scarce and immediately they were put on the counters an enormous queue would form, so I was the scout who would stand in all the queues before returning with the booty.

If I wasn't queueing at the cosmetics counter I was waiting around for cakes, which could be bought off the ration if, again, you were quick enough. Binns was the best shop for this and had gorgeous-looking cakes which were concocted with whatever ingredients were available. If you didn't look too closely, they were a real treat. I would also be sent to the pie shop on Sunderland Bridge at lunchtime with an enormous list. The pies were hot and delicious – until one of the boys from the shipyard told me they were either made from horsemeat or tripe, or both. I'm now sure he just wanted my place in the queue as I was off back to the office as quick as my feet could carry me, and refused to do the 'pie run' ever again!

CHAPTER 4 – EVERY NICE GIRL LOVES A SAILOR!

As the war progressed the Germans switched from bombing London and began to concentrate on places like Liverpool, Hull, Coventry, Bristol and Glasgow – places where industrial production could be severely disrupted and the close-knit communities that existed alongside factories and docks terrorised into submission. Inevitably, Newcastle and Sunderland were prominent on this list, though it wasn't until a few years into the war that we really experienced the big raids.

Up until that point, the war seemed a bit of a game. The blackouts were fun for us youngsters and we didn't mind all the rationing because we weren't rich anyway. In my summer holidays from school I'd be packed off to stay with my Aunt Agnes in Stakeford. She was my father's only known relative so it seemed appropriate to spend time with that side of the family, given that the rest of my life revolved around my mother's people.

This was a great adventure, as it entailed being put on the bus at the Haymarket in Newcastle and travelling the 15 miles to Stakeford alone. I was always nervous that I'd somehow miss the stop for Aunt Agnes's house but luckily that never happened.

When I got there I was greeted by her dog, Gyp, and I adored him. Every day the three of us would go for walks along the banks of the river and among the cornfields, where we would eat a picnic lunch. There were no restrictions on where we could wander, and this being the countryside, we didn't fear any air raids.

Yet the war could intrude into even this quiet part of the North East. One day we were sitting in Aunt Agnes's garden, eating the raspberries we'd just picked. It was a warm afternoon, disturbed only by birdsong and the rattle of the occasional train as it rumbled along the nearby line. Then, I heard a low droning sound. At first I wondered whether it might be a nest of wasps or bees. But as it increased in intensity, the sound was noticeably mechanical.

Auntie and I stared at one another silently. Before we had time to do anything, it seemed like the whole German air force was in the skies above us. They were coming in low towards Newcastle, probably from Norway, and we could clearly see the painted black crosses on the wings, and the dreaded swastika symbol on the tail.

Well, we shot up and dashed into the outside toilet, as there was no air-raid shelter at Auntie's. We dropped to our knees, cowering beneath the deafening roar above, and Auntie prayed loudly, begging Jesus to spare us from the intruders. They seemed to take hours passing over us, but it could only have been a couple of minutes. Still, it was enough to bring out all Auntie's neighbours who stood in the road, shocked, as the squadron headed into the distance. A few moments later we could hear the terrible 'thud, thud' of bombs dropping in the distance, and all I could think about was whether my home and my relatives had been caught up in the horror.

A couple of days later I returned home and my fears were partly realised when I found out that several bombs had landed in the Boldon area. Thankfully, no one I knew had been hurt and the bombing had missed grandma's house. Not surprisingly, there was a fair bit of excitement generated by the raid and Billy Boulton, the enterprising coalman who lived nearby, was giving kids a ride on his lorry to inspect the damage. He swept off the coal dust from the back of the flat-bed truck, put some sacking down and invited all the neighbourhood kids to climb aboard. We travelled around the Boldons and Cleadon, and I couldn't believe how much destruction the raid had caused. Poor Billy – he later joined up and was killed, and they say his wife died of a broken heart. His name is on East Boldon's war memorial.

As I settled into my working life, the raids on the North East became more frequent and deadly. Going home on the bus, especially when it was dark, became downright frightening because of the constant threat of an air raid. I'd stare at the searchlights scanning the sky and pray I'd get home before they caught the bombers in their beams. When I finally came through grandma's door I'd be so relieved, and delighted to see a warming fire in the hearth and my tea on the table. Once inside, it wasn't possible to make arrangements to go out again in case the siren went, so the evenings would be spent knitting or reading. Gran didn't have a radio so we'd go into Auntie Bella's next door to listen to the nine o'clock news. Tommy Handley, star of ITMA ('It's That Man Again!') was very popular and would take our minds off the war.

The darkened streets were generally out of bounds to me, but that didn't go for everyone in my family – particularly Uncle Peter, my Auntie Bella's husband. They'd met while they were both working on a farm and quite soon Bella became pregnant, which grandma wasn't at all happy about as Uncle Peter had form for this particular offence. His name was Peter Thornton Allen and he'd been born into a well-to-do family in South Shields which ran the Moss Empires chain of theatres. He was well-educated, and no doubt set to join the family business when unfortunately he got one of the servant girls pregnant. He left the family home under a cloud, and ended up working on a farm. Auntie Bella was working 'in service' nearby and that's how they met. And as I said, he did the same again....

Anyway, at some stage he was called back to the family home and he dashed away in the assumption that he was due a very big inheritance from his mother. However, he arrived in the middle of a family conference which decided that due to his poor behaviour he wouldn't be entitled to anything. What was rightly his would go to the son he'd fathered with the servant girl. So he came back with his tail between his legs, married Bella and eventually they settled down in East Boldon with their daughter Elsie, who was like a big sister to me. Peter was a lovely man, and never quite lost his 'posh' roots. Even when he was out of work in the Depression he was a member of a gentleman's club and would drink with all the 'high-ups'. Finally, he got a job at Durham County Council and he and Bella seemed happy enough.

That said, Uncle Peter still had an eye for the ladies and during the war he was responsible for maintaining the street barricades that had been erected in case the Germans invaded. The lamps on these had to be lit every night, so he'd go down there to do his duty. One night, as I was walking to church for choir practice with my friend Muriel, I heard a commotion by the barricade, and when I took a closer look there was Auntie Bella knocking the hell out of Mrs Lewthwaite, a local woman. Even as she was hitting her, Auntie Bella was crying her eyes out and I wondered what on earth was going on. Eventually she stopped, and Muriel ran up to the house to fetch Elsie. When we finally got Bella home she was given a glass of whisky and the story began to emerge.

It seemed that Uncle Peter, who was also in the choir and had a lovely tenor voice, had made friends with Mrs Lewthwaite, a fellow choir member whose husband was an ambulance driver at the local hospital. Perhaps she was lonely during the evenings, because she and Uncle Peter seemed to have become closer than they probably should've done. Anyway, Auntie Bella had found out and had taken the law into her own hands. The postscript to this story was that Mrs Lewthwaite didn't quite give up, and began stalking Auntie Bella as she went about her daily business. Of course, the gossip had gone all around the village as quick as wildfire and people felt very sorry for Auntie Bella, especially as Mrs Lewthwaite was now behaving strangely. I had a word with Mr Crossley, a solicitor's clerk at work, and he asked Auntie Bella to come in and 'have a word'. The fee of £15 was spent, a letter was sent to Mrs Lewthwaite and she immediately desisted with her troublemaking. She was warded off – but I'm not sure Uncle Peter ever was! There is a further postscript to the tale of Uncle Peter and his wicked ways, but I will save this for later on in the story.

As for Mr Crossley, well… he was the kind of man who couldn't keep his hands off any passing female and he used to annoy the hell out of us typists with his constant touching, especially if you were bending over for something. I got so fed up with this that I resolved to do something, and next time he pinched me I said, "Stop it! Don't do that or I'll hit you with my cup." He laughed, so I did hit him – and I forgot that my cup was filled with scalding hot tea! Mr Crossley was bald, and my reaction caused him to have a few stitches in his head. He couldn't say much, of course, except that when he returned from the hospital he begged me to tell Mrs Crossley that he'd banged his head on the safe, should she ask!

We all tried to keep cheerful but the winters were hard and cold, and shortages were really beginning to bite. Sometimes we'd stand at the back gate, looking towards the fiery red skies over Sunderland, Newcastle and South Shields, and wonder how all the poor people in those places were possibly managing.

On one occasion the bombing had been particularly heavy and

we were forced to spend the entire night in the Anderson shelter. The Anderson shelter was given by the county council and arrived in parts which were installed by the family in the garden. Because there were three families sharing a garden we erected it (ten feet in the ground) as a communal shelter for the three families. There were seven of us and a baby (so eight all together) – me, grandma, Auntie Bella, Uncle Peter, and our neighbours Mr and Mrs Gibson with their daughter Millie and her baby – Millie's husband was away in the army in Burma. We were very relieved when the 'All Clear' sounded and were able to climb out into the fresh morning air. I went back into the house, changed into a very pretty blue dress, which I was very proud of, and headed off on the train to work. As we approached Sunderland Station we were told it had received a direct hit and that we would have to get out and walk the rest of the way. As I hurried into the city, hoping not to be late, I could not believe what I was seeing. There were piles of rubble everywhere and fires still smouldering among the wreckage. Tiptoeing over the broken glass and edging my way around the shrapnel scattered all around, I tried to get to my office in John Street by the normal route. Then a Warden stopped me in my tracks.

"Where are you going?" he said, his palm up towards me.

"I'm trying to get to work," I said. "In John Street. Can I pass through?"

The warden laughed and asked me what number MacKenzie and Co was at. I replied that it was 66.

"I'm sorry to tell you that it received a direct hit," he said. "You're welcome to go on through but I'll warn you, hinny, there isn't much left."

With that, he stood aside and let me pass. As I walked down the street my blood ran cold. Most of the office buildings and the church opposite were flattened. My workplace was just about standing, but without its frontage. There were files and bits of broken office furniture all over the place. I thought about my male colleagues who had volunteered to fire-watch that night. What had happened to them?

As I stood, open-mouthed, my boss came around the corner. What he saw stopped him in his tracks. He must have been in complete shock, because he came up to me and, with a business-like tone of voice, said, "Well, we can't just stand here. We must see what we can do."

"How do you mean?" I said.

"Perhaps you could go in there, Miss Armstrong," he replied, "and see what you can retrieve. You might be able to locate yesterday's post, and find a typewriter that works."

Today I'd think, 'what a fool!' But I was young, and we did what we were told. However, just as I was entering the building, a warden nearby yelled at me at the top of his voice.

"What do you think you're doing?!" he screamed. "Come out of there- it's very dangerous!"

That brought me to my senses. Everything was wrecked and we'd have to start again somewhere else. We did locate a typewriter that had fallen out of a window but it was beyond repair. If it hadn't been, I think my boss would have had me typing there and then!

After rescuing what documents we could, he and I walked down the street. Some people from a nearby law firm that somehow had been undamaged offered us a room, and that's where our firm was located for the next three years while repairs were carried out. Other staff joined us and we spent the rest of the day gingerly pulling bits and pieces from the rubble. I went home completely covered in grime and dust, and when I walked through the door my grandma nearly had a fit.

"That beautiful blue dress!" she shouted, "totally ruined! You should've been watching what you were doing!"

Never mind Hitler, it seemed I was completely to blame for

the dress turning from blue to black!

Sadly, we discovered that the boys who were fire watching were killed, as was the vicar of the church that was flattened. That news was terrible for us, but by this stage in the war we all knew boys who'd gone out to fight and hadn't come back. The thought of those young men whose lives were lost upsets me to this day.

Recently, I went with my daughter-in-law, Bella, to London. I'd seen pictures of the Bomber Command Memorial in Green Park and very much wanted to visit it. It took a long time, and a lot of persuasion, to have this memorial built to the 50,000 aircrew who were killed in the war. Some people claim that the bombing campaign over Germany was controversial, but I say that if it hadn't happened we'd have been living under the swastika.

Anyway, we went along to look at it and something about the way the aircrew had been sculpted looking up into the sky brought back memories of a lad I knew at MacKenzie and Co, whose name was Amos Maddison. Amos was an office boy who'd been promoted and he sat next to me. He was good fun and all the time I knew him he was desperate to join the air force. He used to hold his pen nib down, then drop it on to the desk and say, "This is how we'll bomb Germany!" I was 16, if that, and I was probably a bit sweet on him. Not that he ever knew.

He got his wish and was accepted into the Royal Canadian Air Force, where he trained as a rear gunner, becoming a Flight Sergeant. He sent me a picture of himself sitting on the wing of a plane with his mates, all looking up into the sky, just like the statue, and when he came home on leave he called in at the office and asked if I wanted to go to the cinema with him.

Did I just!? That day I had a lovely new riding mackintosh on and I felt very trendy. So off we went to the Havelock Cinema, on the corner of Fawcett Street and High Street West, and afterwards we went for a toasted teacake at a teashop, which is what we always liked to do when Amos was working in the office. As we got up to leave, the pocket of my new mac became caught on a door handle and ripped. I could've wept, but Amos was very calm. "Never mind, Olive," he said, "let's nip back into the office and we'll put some tape on it from the first aid box." It was about 6.30pm and no one was around, so we went in and Amos taped it up for me. Then we said goodnight and off I went home.

A few days later I was back at the office when there was a knock at the little hatch on the door, which was used to take the mail in. I opened it, and standing there was Amos's sister, looking ashen-faced.

"I've got a message for Mr Watts," she said. Mr Watts was Amos's old boss.

"Oh yes?" I said. "What is it?"

"Can you tell him we've just got word that Amos was killed yesterday."

Speechless, I just stared at her. I can't even remember what I said, if anything. I was in complete shock. Later, I was told that a few hours after we'd said goodnight he received a telegram ordering him to immediately return to his base at RAF Dishforth in North Yorkshire, as he and his crew were needed to take part in a raid.

It was the evening of January 14, 1943, and the six-man crew (including Amos) of a Wellington bomber took off from Dishforth and, with 121 other aircraft, headed for Lorient, a French port which was used by the Nazis as a U-boat base. The plan was to put the thing out of use, but it wasn't a successful raid and 12 local people were killed, with 120 buildings destroyed in the town centre.

The U-boat base was heavily fortified and defended, and somewhere in the Bay of Biscay Amos's aircraft was shot down by flak. It was never found, and no bodies were recovered. And that was the end of Amos, along with so many other local boys who joined the air force and were killed on missions like this. Which is why, seventy-odd years later, I was standing in front of the Bomber Command memorial with tears running down my face.

Bella looked at me in surprise. "Why are you crying?" she said. She knows I'm not a crier. So I told her the story of Amos, just 20 years old when he was killed, and how this statue reminded me of the photo of my lost friend and his mates. It's hard to believe that it took so long to put up a memorial to them. It's shameful, when you think about it. They were almost forgotten.

While doing research for the book we came across Amos' medals being sold online – unfortunately we were too late to be able to buy them as they had already been sold, but it was a poignant moment. This photo is a screenshot from http://www.harlandmilitaryantiques.co.uk.

You can only imagine how Mrs Maddison must have felt receiving these medals and what a shame that they did not stay in the Maddison extended family, but maybe there are no family members who would remember him? Maybe I am the only person still alive who remembers him? Well, I do remember and I hope that by including him in my book he will be remembered by everyone who reads this; and who knows, one day the person who bought his medals may see this book and learn a little bit more about the young man who was so much more than just a name on a certificate or a war memorial.

All sorts of things happened during the war that you'd just take in your stride. I remember sitting on the bus going home one evening when a huge aircraft swooped in low, just above us, and crashed right on to the railway line, just by the Boldon Greyhound Stadium. It was a British plane and must have been coming back from a raid. The bus stopped suddenly and all the male passengers got out and ran over the field to see if they could help. After a few minutes the bus continued its journey as though nothing had happened. That's how it was back then.

At least we were 'all in it together', as they said, and the bonds forged between people who went through similar experiences were very strong indeed. I had many friends during the war, not least Muriel Pendlington, Doreen Joliffe and Diana Basham. We were all at school together and later we all joined our church choir. Some of our happiest times were spent going to the pictures and to parties and dances, all the while trying to ape the American film stars by smoking!

My gran, of course, was Victorian both by birth and in her attitudes and in the later war years we were often at loggerheads over the amount of fun I was attempting to have. Today I'd be described as a rebellious teenager but even the term 'teenager' was unheard of then. I was just 'cheeky' and by rights I should 'be seen and not heard'. I was lucky in that, although clothing was rationed, grandma never bought herself anything so I got all her coupons instead. Even so, I still needed money to pay for clothes and gran had her own form of rationing over my wages. Basically, I handed everything over and she gave me my bus fares and a little for pocket money. As a teenage girl it was never enough and although I had extra coupons I was never out of grandma's debt.

When clothes were bought it was always on a 'club', which limited where you spent your money. On rare occasions grandma gave me a bit extra to buy a nice dress in Sunderland, and it was lovely trying on clothes that didn't come from the local Co-op. Steadily I built up a nice wardrobe of items which gran forbade me to wear, except for 'best' and on Sundays. So I would invent places I had to go, perhaps with my job, during the week, but even then I was only allowed to wear my 'second best' clothes. I made the best of it, though it was very frustrating at times.

I mentioned that a lot of us girls were in the choir at St George's in East Boldon, which was my local church. We would practice during the week and sing three times on a Sunday. Before Evensong, grandma would make us both Sunday tea. She'd remove the tablecloth she used during the week and replace it with a green chenille one, complete with tassels. When we finished our tea and cake she'd locate her hat, gloves and prayer book and place them on the table in preparation for the Sunday service. Interestingly, gran was born a Roman Catholic but never let on to anyone about that, and happily attended Communion at a C of E church.

My friend Diana was a good pianist and she'd sometimes play the organ in church. However, it wasn't always hymns she played, as we found out when a few of us went to look at the new organ that had recently been installed in the church. No one else was in the church, so Diana decided to give it a test drive by playing a selection of jazz and swing standards. Of course, this was the pop music of the day so we were all swaying and jiving to the rhythm when, as if from nowhere, the vicar appeared. The syncopated notes died away as he approached and asked us, kindly enough, to come down from the organ loft.

Shame-faced we trooped down the steps. He must have seen how embarrassed we were because he didn't seem too cross. He just said something about not playing 'that sort of music in God's house.' Then he invited us all to tea the following Thursday to 'have a little chat' about what we'd done. Dutifully we went along on the appointed date and enjoyed his hospitality – and jazz wasn't even mentioned.

As we got a little older the attractions of the choir began to wane somewhat and occasionally a handful of us would go to the pictures on a Sunday night instead. We felt so guilty for doing this, and we'd have been in trouble if we'd been caught. But we were young and even though it was wartime and so many dreadful things were happening, we just wanted a good time.

Now, to turn the clock back just a little bit, I should mention that at age 14 I was allowed to go with Auntie Bella to the Mothers' Union Whist Drive and Dance at the Parish Hall, which was only two doors up from where I lived. These sound boring affairs and I'm afraid that they were just that! I would usually wash up after the supper was finished and before the dancing started. One of these evenings I was standing there, watching people dance and wondering how it was done, when I spotted a lady I knew with her son, who was in Naval uniform, complete with little round hat and bell-bottomed trousers.

He was only young, no more than 18 or 19, but he was confident enough to stride over and ask me if I wanted to dance. "Well," I said, a bit taken aback, "I don't know. I'll have to ask Auntie Bella."

Auntie Bella laughed when I asked her. She knew my life with grandma could be restrictive at times, so she told me to go on and enjoy myself. And I danced with this young sailor, who introduced himself as Ronnie Roberts, and we chatted quite happily. When the dance was finished he asked if he could walk me home.

"I'm going away for three years soon," he said. "Maybe you'll write to me…?"

Now, as I've mentioned, I only lived two doors from the Parish Hall so it wasn't going to be the longest romantic stroll ever. But when Auntie Bella gave me permission for Ronnie to walk me home, I decided to take the 'long route' – past grandma's, down the street and as far as the railway station. Eventually, Ronnie asked where I lived and when I said, 'next to the Parish Hall' he laughed heartily.

We walked back and sat for a while on a low wall opposite my house. As we were chatting I noticed our front door opening slightly, throwing a chink of light into the blacked-out street. Next second, out she came – grandma, wearing a white pinny and an expression of thunder across her face. She disappeared back inside for a second and re-emerged with a long brush with feathers on it.

"Come here, you!" she shouted, "and get inside. Sitting on the streets with sailors at ten o'clock at night. You'll come to a bad end!"

I didn't even have time to say goodbye to Ronnie Roberts, for she chased me inside and then pursued me round the kitchen table with the feather brush. As usual, she didn't catch me but she made her point and, despite my protests that he was going away for three years (to which she shouted "Good!!"), that was the end of the matter as far as she was concerned.

I was unable to give Ronnie Roberts my address so that he could write to me, so I had no idea how his war would play out. Well, not until after it had finished anyway, because later on this man became my husband and the love of my life.

Now, to jump forward in time… some years ago our son Nigel set us up on a computer so that we could use the internet and type up any stories we had from the past. We both managed quite a number of words, but ill health put a stop to Ronnie's account of his life. That said, for the next chapter I'd like to bring his words and his voice into my story and let him talk about his own background, childhood and the moment he and I met at the Parish Hall.

CHAPTER 5 – RON'S BEGINNINGS

I was born on June 11, 1925, the son of Moses Roberts and Jane Phalp Roberts (nee Anderson) at 2 St Nicholas Terrace, West Boldon, and christened at St Nicholas Church, in the same village. My father had three sons by a previous marriage – William, Frederick and Arthur – while my mother had a daughter called Edna Jane.

At the time I was born my father had retired from mining and was running a fruiterer's business, along with an ice cream business in the summer months. He died in 1931, when I was just five years old, and later I learned his business had failed because of the hard times that followed the 1926 miners' strike. After that business failure, everything had to be sold, including our furniture, and we moved to a very small house in Hylton Road, West Boldon.

Most of the proceeds of the sale went towards financing my two elder brothers to get a new start in London. The remainder went very quickly as my father succumbed to silicosis contracted when he was a miner. To help him breathe more easily he and two friends, also suffering from the same disease, used to take a daily 'constitutional' up Hylton Bank as far as the reservoir. But his illness became worse and eventually he was taken to Gilsland Sanatorium for rest and recuperation.

When he returned home I had already started at the C of E school in

West Boldon. I didn't realise he was ill and to me, life seemed fine. We enjoyed our regular Sunday night gatherings, which neighbours and friends would attend and all would sing songs, accompanied by my brother Arthur on the cottage organ, followed by tea and biscuits. My party piece was to stand on a 'cracket' (a form of stool) and sing, 'My cup is full and running over'.

Towards the close of the first term at school, my father was confined to bed. He lasted the Christmas holidays but by January he was dead. I recall being taken into the bedroom and seeing my dad in a box with a frilly, shiny pillow. On the day of the funeral the house was quite crowded, everyone standing around the coffin singing 'The Old Rugged Cross'. I was standing in front of my brother Fred, his hands on my shoulders and his tears dropping on to my head.

Not long after this my sister Edna was taken ill and was confined in Stannington Sanatorium, where she remained for about a year. It was a long way from Boldon and expensive to get there by bus. My mother had to go alone because she could not afford to take me with her. However, the local rector's niece, whom we called 'Miss Marjorie', would take us in the rector's car and as this was the only one in the village, the thrill of riding in a motor was indescribable - I was the envy of my friends. On these occasions I was only able to speak to my sister through a glass screen because she was in isolation with suspected TB. Then mum would stay with Edna while Miss Marjorie took me around Morpeth (little did I know my future wife was probably living there then). We wandered through the streets until we came to Woolworths, and I remember Miss Marjorie buying me a popgun from there. It was the most wonderful present I'd had in a long time.

After she was released from the sanatorium Edna worked at Gibson's Farm, right next door to us. That was great for me as it gave me the privilege of riding on the hay bogeys, and earning a few coppers getting the cows in, driving a horse and cart in the harvest time, and helping to build the hay and corn stacks. It seemed that in those days the sun always shone and life was wonderful.

The time came for me to take the eleven-plus exam that would get me into the secondary school in Washington. I passed the first half but failed the second part at Washington because they asked me a question about algebra and I'd never heard of it. So unlike the businessmen's sons who could afford extra tuition to pass the exam, I was left behind to finish school at the local C of E. Still, I enjoyed it until I got into the top class and was taught by the headmaster, a man named Mark Wilson. To me he was despicable because he seemed to enjoy caning children, and while I wasn't on the receiving end, a couple of boys he classed as 'backward' were regular victims. I can still see him preparing to give some poor child six of the best. He would call the unfortunate boy to the front of the class, get the came from the cupboard, flex it, have a couple of swishes into thin air, put the cane down, lick the palms of his hands and smooth his bushy eyebrows back. Then he'd say, "This will teach you, lad," take up the cane and do his worst.

Of course, we never dared fight back but we had a little ditty about him that kept us going through the worst of times:

"Markie Wilson's a very good man, he goes to church on Sundays/ To pray to God to give him strength, to whack the kids on Mondays."

In 1937, I think, we moved house from Hylton Road to 51 Addison Road. This was a newly built council house and it seemed the last word in luxury. We had two bedrooms upstairs and a bath with hot and cold running water, albeit that the hot had to be topped up with water from a boiling kettle to keep it at least tepid! Downstairs we had the kitchen with a tiled hearth, a coal fire with an inefficient back boiler and a cupboard under the stairs for the gas meter. There was a gas oven and a sink with hot and cold taps and a drainer. In the back passage (and that does not mean what you may think it means!), luxury of luxury, we had an indoor coal house and WC. My mum's income at that time was 15 shillings a week (widow's pension) and the rent was five bob. I never lacked for anything and it was not until many years later that it even occurred to me how much mum must've done without.

When I was 12 I was confirmed into the Church of England by the Bishop of Durham. I had always attended Sunday School regularly but this was the beginning of my religious period. I first became a choir boy but it did not take them long to find out that, even with my Welsh ancestry, I was no singer. I was posted to the job of acolyte and as soon as I had had a bit of experience at the altar, I was appointed a server. Before I could wear the red cassock and white surplice I had to learn the format of Holy Communion and Sung Eucharist, plus the responses, with great care. The head server, Bobby Sutton, taught me how to lay out the Rector's robes for the different seasons of the Church, a task that took me weeks to master.

I was looking forward to leaving school on my 14ᵗʰ birthday, June 11, 1939, but just before it happened, the school leaving age was raised on a voluntary basis to 15 and my mum decided I would stay on, much to my disappointment. She reckoned an extra year at school would do me no harm and although I'd have liked a job in the pit or the shipyard, perhaps she thought that the five-bob portion of the pension she got for me was more than I was likely to earn.

The final year at school wasn't a happy one, although I did attend night school and was taught more about English and Maths than I'd ever learned at the C of E school. During that year, a scheme was introduced to take poorer children to a holiday camp in Cresswell. The girls would go first and we boys would follow on their return. Arrangements were made well in advance, with a lot of form-filling to be done, but I was very excited to be going, until... It so happened that some samples of PK chewing gum were stored in the school staff room and somehow a handful of kids from class ended up there, including me. Two class members found the gum and helped themselves to it. I was too scared to take any but was threatened with a good hiding by one of the thieves if I told anyone.

Inevitably the theft was discovered and we were all threatened with the cane unless someone confessed. One of the thieves accused me, and after a bit of persuasion I told the truth and gave away the identity of the real culprits. Unfortunately I was not believed, and the head teacher said I could choose one of two punishments – either forfeit the holiday to Cresswell or leave school without a reference. I remember thinking that 'Mam will kill me if she finds out' so I opted for the lack of a reference. My leaving date was six months away and that seemed forever.

As it was, the growing fears about another war breaking out saw the holiday cancelled, but Mr Wilson, our sadistic headmaster, refused to waive the no-reference punishment. I have never forgiven him for the injustice of not being believed. However, when I eventually told my mum she went in to bat for me and made the person who'd blamed me tell the truth to Mr Wilson. Even then he refused to give in so mum enlisted the help of the Rector, and finally Wilson was called upon to apologise to mum — and I received a glowing reference from the Rector.

That final year at school saw all the preparations being made for war. By now it was inevitable, and there would be no 'peace for our time', as Chamberlain had promised. Anderson shelters were delivered to every home and because mum was a widow, two men from the council were sent to erect ours. They dug a deep hole and placed corrugated metal sheets with bars and bolts inside the hole. After that, they threw all the excavated soil and clay back on top of the shelter. For me, it became a fascinating place to play, and I'd go down there with friends to tell ghost stories until we scared ourselves half to death!

The day war was declared I was serving for the Rector at the eleven o'clock service. The service had just got underway when the churchwarden, Mr Ritchies, came up the aisle and whispered in the Rector's ear. The Rector turned to the congregation and said:

"I'm afraid to say that war has just been declared, and those who wish may leave the church now."

Then, in a stage whisper, he added: "That does not mean you, Ronnie Roberts!"

Ten minutes later, Mr Ritchies came back to say the air raid siren was going, and again the Rector made his offer to anyone who wanted to leave. Now, pretty much anyone who was left after the first announcement rose to take their leave, but again the Rector insisted that I stayed. We went through the entire service, sermon and all, and later I learned I'd missed out on a lot of fun. It seemed that a neighbour had panicked at the idea she could smell gas, and her entire family had been urged to don their gas masks. It took them a long time to live that down!

When I left school in the summer of 1940, I landed a job with the North East Electricity Supply Company, known as NESCO. I travelled to East

Boldon in my best suit but was brought back down to earth when my first job was to dust the shelves in the showroom. Quickly, I learned that the role of office boy was the lowest of the low, at everyone's beck and call. All I seemed to do was run, fetch and carry and within weeks I was completely bored. I stuck it for nine months before deciding that even the shipyards would be better, so I applied, and got an apprenticeship as a coppersmith at the Sir James Laing shipyard in Sunderland.

I really enjoyed learning to bash sheets of copper into pipes, and braze the edges together on a furnace. I would fill copper pipes with molten pitch and when it had set, bend the pipes to the shape of the template on a big hand-operated machine. I cycled to work and that meant an early start as we clocked on at 7.30am. If you arrived after the hooter blew you could not clock on for 15 minutes and that meant lost pay.

The pipe bender that I mentioned above was supported on chocks, and one day, when I was helping to manhandle a large pipe, a chock slipped and the machine crushed my left big toe. The foreman decided I would have to go to hospital to have it checked but I did not have the luxury of an ambulance. Instead, the foreman co-opted a friend from Boldon to accompany me on our bikes. The joint turned out to be crushed and I was told to stay at home for three weeks. The shipyard gave me injury benefit while I was off work, but before I could be paid I had to sign a form saying this would be in full settlement for my injury – and I was daft enough to sign. Later, I learned that in addition to the injury benefit that would keep me going while I was off work, I could also have claimed a bigger compensation for the injury itself, that from time-to-time bothered me for the rest of my life.

I only lasted a couple of years at the shipyard because I was experiencing severe pains in the stomach and my doctor decided it was related to fumes. I couldn't just leave, however, as the job was a reserved occupation and I was an indentured apprentice. So I was released after a medical, and the significance of the stomach pains will come later on in my story.

While I was at the shipyard, and before I joined up, I had to help the war effort on the home front, so I joined the Auxiliary Fire Service (AFS) as a messenger. The AFS was manned by full and part-time staff. I was only a part-timer but after work we used to report to the fire station for training and standby duties. When the siren sounded we had to report immediately unless we were at work. The fire station was the pre-war village billiard hall and a couple of tables had been left behind, so we had a great time playing billiards and snooker when we were on standby. I think that was the main reason I joined the AFS because my mother thought it was only rogues and layabouts who ventured into snooker halls!

If the siren sounded I used to supervise mam and her neighbours, the Moores, into the air-raid shelter. The reason this was my responsibility was that Mr Moore was Head Warden and had to be on duty right away. It used to be quite a hassle as Mrs Moore had two young children and we had to sort out all the gas masks and blankets because they would become damp if left in the shelter in advance. I also boiled the kettle for flasks of hot water and when this was done, mam would insist I get her box of policies from under the bed. Often by this time the guns were firing and bits of shrapnel could be heard whistling by.

On one such night with all my jobs done I headed off towards the fire station. On the way I met my pal Gordon Edgerton and when we got as far as the air-raid shelter all hell was let loose. Mr Moore grabbed us and insisted we stay until things had quietened down. Gordon was an ARP messenger and his HQ was just a short way through the churchyard to the Mansion House. After a while he dashed off, saying that he'd be alright. He had not been away a couple of minutes when a huge explosion indicated a bomb had landed nearby.

Eventually it quietened down and I was allowed to proceed to the fire station. Once there I found all the appliances were out and the station officer and telephone operator the building's only occupants. They told me there had been terrible bombing at South Shields and all the telephones were knocked out. The station commander said he needed to know of the situation so that any returning appliances would be dispatched to South Shields immediately. So I was asked to cycle to South Shields, find the leading fireman and get a reply to the commander's note.

Off I went and although it was only four miles I did not make fast progress because of the rubble on the roads. I was not scared – just absolutely terrified! I found the leading fireman, a Mr King. He read the note and told me to get the hell out of there, and to tell the station commander he must be 'off his rocker' for sending a kid out in such a raid. I got back safely and the raid ended.

Next day we learned that Gordon Edgerton had been killed by a bomb that had fallen in the churchyard, and in Shields market place there had been an underground shelter that had received a direct hit. Many people were trapped but all rescue attempts failed and eventually the bomb crater was just filled in and the bodies left there.

On another occasion the Germans were bombing Sunderland and this time I went on a fire tender to the incident. A bomb had destroyed the Bon Marche cinema, which was right on the end of Sunderland Bridge. Many people had been sheltering in its cellar and not many were rescued. I stayed in the tender all the time as there were no messages for me to carry. I was aware that Sunderland had been hit badly, including the railway station and John Street. I did not know it then, of course, but next morning my future wife was searching her bombed-out office for the mail, typewriters and anything she could salvage.

Once free of the shipyard I immediately volunteered for the RAF and passed the medical. Previously I'd been in the Air Training Corps, and this really helped my application. I wanted to be a pilot (who didn't?) but I failed the selection board and was accepted as a trainee Wireless Operator/Airgunner (WOP/AG). I'd learned to read Morse in the ATC and by the time I went to Wireless Training College in Blackpool I could read it at 18 words a minute – considered good for a beginner.

'Initial Training' in Blackpool was the euphemism for square-bashing, but at least we were billeted away from camp. Mine was a boarding house in Hornby Road. I must have liked it because years later Olive and I spent our honeymoon there. That second time, though, I wasn't quite as impressed as I had been during the war. The great thing about being billeted out was that unless you were on guard duties or fire-watching you were a free man from the last parade of the day until curfew, which was 9.30pm. We square-bashed on the prom, took part in assault courses in Stanley Park and swam at Derby Baths.

The wireless school was on the upper floor of a big Burtons shop in the centre of town. A weekly test determined whether you passed or failed, and if it was the latter it was said that you'd 'gone for a Burton', which is where I believe the saying originated.

I was having a wonderful time in Blackpool until one day when we were summoned to parade in the Tower Ballroom. Our Group Commander told us he wanted 150 volunteers to go into the Royal Navy for a special job, and anyone wishing to volunteer should take three paces forward. Well, after a bit of shuffling only half a dozen men came forward. The 'Groopy' was a decisive chap and told the Warrant Officer to make every third rank take three paces forward. They were duly counted and secretly I was celebrating. Because I was tall I'd been made a 'marker', meaning I was in the first rank and therefore would not be chosen.

Unfortunately, my luck ran out. The Groopy realised there were six men short, and among the six replacements was me. I was very disappointed, but as I had volunteered for the RAF I knew I could be asked to be discharged until my proper call-up time came. I went to see the WO and he listened quite patiently. Then when I'd finished he looked at me and uttered the dread words:

"Right lad, you can go if you want to but I will make sure you end up in the Pioneer Corps."

And from that moment I became a very enthusiastic sailor!

Soon after, all 150 of us were dispatched to HMS Royal Arthur. We couldn't believe we were to board a ship right away – and we were right not to believe it. HMS Royal Arthur was actually the Butlins Holiday Camp in Skegness, which had been requisitioned for the duration by the War Ministry. We were given various pep talks before being kitted out with our naval uniforms. They seemed incredibly tight, compared to our RAF clobber, and with kit bags full and new tin helmets strapped to our gas masks we were marched off to be taught how to sling a hammock. If you hadn't learned that by the time you'd left Skegness you would not get many nights' sleep.

We were all on a telegraphists' course and I really enjoyed it. Radio training was much more thorough in the Royal Navy and we were also taught how to send and read semaphore, Aldis lamp and flag signals. After my fourth weekly exam I was made Acting Telegraphist and given a small raise in pay. After eight weeks I was drafted to Petersfield, Hampshire, where there was a big Naval Radio College. Here I continued my training and other unpleasant things like square-bashing, fatigues and guard duties. The morning watch - 0400 to 0600 — was very popular because we got to go into the WRENS' quarters to wake up the cooks. Some of those girls were pretty hard cases.

Eventually I became a Telegraphist Trained Operator (TEL/TO) and I was drafted to another land-based ship at Fareham, HMS Collingwood. I was given seven days' leave and a rail warrant to get me home, and I had to go through London to catch the train to the North East. Seeing the capital in such a state of devastation due to bombing was a terrible shock. Finally I arrived home to Boldon and was paraded in my uniform all over the place by my proud mother, as I was the only sailor in the area. On the Thursday night of that week I went to the Whist Drive and Dance, and it was here that I became friendly with a young girl called Olive. I plucked up courage and asked to walk her home, and she agreed.

After the last dance we got our coats and went off walking as far as Blacks Corner. Once there, Olive said we would have to go back again as she lived up the village, so off we went; back to the house next door to the Parish Hall. We sat on a wall outside her house and I was telling her I had to report back to my ship next day (keeping quiet the fact that it was a land-based vessel!) when an elderly lady suddenly appeared waving a feather duster. She was demanding to know what Olive was doing with a sailor 'at this time of night' and within seconds Olive was chased indoors. I was quite concerned, but bravely peeped through the window to see this girl being chased around the kitchen table, the old lady with the feather duster in hot pursuit. And that was the last I saw of Olive for a good while!

Chapter 6 – The Wanderer Returns

I liked Ronnie Roberts, but at that point he was just another lad in the village. So many of them were now in uniform and going here, there and everywhere that I wasn't particularly bothered about getting attached to one. And as I hadn't even had time to say goodbye to Ronnie, I couldn't be getting attached to him!

Life went on as normal – or as normal as life could be in wartime. As I've said, my friends and I were all young, lively women and, war or not, we just wanted to go out to dance, wear nice clothes, get made up and have fun. The battles with my grandma continued but in the back of my mind I knew how much she'd sacrificed for me, and although our arguments were frequent we never fell out for any length of time.

Local boys in uniform were one thing, but when the American and Canadian airmen arrived with their good looks and film-star accents – well, our quiet little village was never the same again. There was a dance every Friday night in the local YMCA hall and we'd go along never knowing who'd be there. As well as the Americans and Canadians there were Scottish soldiers, troops from the ammunition dump in Boldon and airmen from

Usworth. My friend Muriel and I would get ourselves all dressed up and, with 'tan' on our legs (usually gravy browning) and our hair done up Betty Grable style, we'd saunter forth, feeling a million dollars and ready to sample the local and foreign talent.

The Scots were fun, but you had to be careful of them after they'd had a drink. I remember the Black Watch being billeted close by following a spell fighting in the desert, and they went absolutely mad on the booze. Then there were the black American airmen, who arrived later in the war. Us locals had had a sheltered life and up until the war I'd never seen a black person, apart from the occasional Arab in South Shields. So when one of these young men asked me to dance one evening, my immediate reaction was horror, probably driven by fear. I feel awful now when I think back to that. But I'd no experience of meeting anyone other than white people. Still, I accepted his invitation, danced with him, and realised he was a human being just like anyone else.

We got up to all sorts of silly things. I remember walking past a group of soldiers with my friend Doreen and one of them gave us two oranges. These were a rarity of course, but instead of doing the sensible thing and eating them for their Vitamin C content, Doreen suggested we squeeze them and rub the juice in our hair.

"It'll make us blonde!" she said, excitedly.

"That's lemons, you daft thing," I said. "Not oranges!"

But Doreen was insistent, so we went to her house, squeezed the juice and spent the next 10 minutes vigorously rubbing it into our hair. Then we waited… and waited… and waited. And nothing happened!

As well as dances we were frequent attendees at the cinema. I barely missed a picture in those days. Every week would see us queuing up at either the Ritz or the Regal to see the latest Hollywood movie. If we could get someone to take us and pay for us, so much the better. We sometimes tested the waters in

Sunderland, taking in a movie and a dance. Many times we missed the last bus back and had to walk back to Boldon, a distance of some seven miles in the blackout. We were never afraid and became quite blasé about air raids. Often the sky would be lit up by searchlights and we'd see German aircraft weaving about, trying to dodge them. Then the guns would start up, which would make us run the last mile or two. Even so, it was exciting to be a part of. I remember being in Sunderland one day, enjoying a bit of shopping, when, as one, a crowd of people all started to look upwards. I looked up too, and there was a dogfight going on between a German and a British plane. It was hard to imagine that thousands of feet up in the sky, two people were trying to kill each other, and when one plane finally crashed into the sea we all cheered. I don't know if it was the British or the German aircraft, but we cheered all the same. It was a strange time to be alive, that's for sure.

As we know, by the end of 1944 the tide of war had turned in the Allies' favour and by mid-1945 it was all over. I remember the excitement we all felt on May 7, 1945. This was the day before VE Day and although we knew it was over, the end of the war still had to be officially declared. Even so, all the flags and bunting were out in East Boldon and even my undemonstrative grandmother had allowed her cottage to be done up in red, white and blue flags. That was a shock, and I can only guess that my Uncle Peter 'liberated' all these decorations from Durham County Council, where he worked as a storeman, and somehow persuaded grandma to allow them to be displayed.

On VE Day itself Muriel and I went into Sunderland, where there were wild celebrations. Bands were playing along Fawcett Street and we danced and sang non-stop, kissing everyone we met. We joined long chains of people dancing the Conga, in circles doing the Hokey-Cokey and in long lines doing the Palais Glide. The shipyards weren't working that day and all the lads had been let out to join the party. During the war, it was always the boys in uniforms who got the girls and the shipyard lads felt they'd missed out. So on VE Day they really made up for lost time and they were hilarious with it.

After all this excitement we caught the bus home, packed full of people merry in all sorts of ways, and in the evening we borrowed some 'posh frocks' (I think mine might have been a bridesmaid's dress) and went to the YMCA for the biggest party the village had seen in many years. Months later, around December, there was a special service in the church to celebrate the first Christmas of peacetime. All the lights were on now and the big stained-glass windows were lit up like Christmas trees. There were people in uniform from all over the world in the church that night, and every pew was full. The choir, of which I was still a part, sang 'Hark The Herald Angels Sing' and it was a very emotional moment indeed, not least when I thought of those local boys, and the ones I'd worked with in Sunderland, who wouldn't be coming home. I thought about them then, and I think of them now.

After Ronnie Roberts departed to shores unknown, I dated a few boys, mainly British, but I wasn't serious about anyone. However, I had been writing to a lad from Glasgow who was in the Navy, a friend of a friend's brother. His name was Jimmy Swan, and he was a humorous boy who liked a drink and used to sing all sorts of songs. We kept in touch during the later years of the war and there was talk of a possible engagement, which I think my grandmother was keen on. Just after the war ended, he arrived back in East Boldon and was waiting to be demobbed, which meant that he'd have to go to one of the big Naval bases down south, Portsmouth or Plymouth, I think. Eventually his number came up and he headed off to the south coast, telling he'd be back once he had his discharge papers.

We still went to dances every Friday night – because there were many servicemen around who were also waiting to be demobbed, or in transit somewhere else – and one of these nights, as I walked into the hall, I noticed a sailor dancing with a local girl. As I watched them, a feeling that I'd seen him somewhere before nagged at me. Then I realised – it was the boy who'd walked me home after the Whist Drive and Dance and had scarpered when grandma had waved her feather duster at him. I was now 18 and he was 21, and we'd both changed a bit, but I was certain of his identity. I nudged my friend Muriel.

"That's him!" I said. "The lad who walked me home that night. Ronnie someone… Ronnie Roberts. That's him. He's back!"

Then we realised that the dance currently taking place was a Ladies Excuse-Me. This meant that any girl could suddenly cut into a dancing couple and waltz off with the man. This was known as 'buzzing off'. Perhaps the Excuse-Me was invented to give the shyer girls a chance to enjoy a few moments in a boy's arms.

"Go on then, Olive," Muriel urged. "Buzz her off and tell him who you are!"

Bold as brass I went up, touched the girl on the shoulder and she dutifully complied with my request. I danced with Ronnie, who started telling me something about his adventures in the Navy. He seemed to have really travelled the world, having been in India, Ceylon, Singapore and various other places, and all the while I smiled at him, realising that he had absolutely no idea who I was.

The dance finished and we went our separate ways. Then about 20 minutes later he came over and asked if I wanted to dance again. I accepted, and we danced the night away. He still didn't seem to recognise me and so I said nothing. Then he asked to walk me home and I thought, 'Now he'll remember…' But still he didn't.

I liked him, and I was pleased when he asked me for a date the following day. I accepted the offer, and so he went towards the bus stop for West Boldon while I entered grandma's house, braced for the inevitable grilling.

Now, this is going to be a short chapter because I'm going to let Ron take over and talk about his life on active service – and how the penny eventually dropped over my identity!

CHAPTER 7 – RON'S WAR

After my leave I arrived back in Fareham to find British and American soldiers everywhere, along with all their equipment and armoury. It was late May 1944 and something huge was about to happen, but we didn't know what. Finally, I was told what my 'special job' was going to be - a Telegraphist on a Motor Torpedo Boat. We were in for some intensive training and my first experience at sea was on one of these vessels.

Our mission was to seek out German 'E boats' (their equivalent of our MTB) and send them to the bottom of the English Channel. In the training period I didn't see anything, not even a fishing boat, until we were sent out in the middle of the night to patrol a set area. As dawn broke I saw a sight I shall never forget; hundreds, maybe thousands, of ships of all kinds were everywhere as far as the eye could see, and the sky was filled with bombers and fighters.

It was June 6, 1944 – D Day. All hell was let loose when the battleships and destroyers opened up with their guns and the bombs fell on the German fortifications along the French coast. As the day progressed we saw many British ships burning and sinking, along with many bodies in the water. Our skipper said we should not try to rescue anyone as the Germans may have booby-trapped the bodies. We saw only one German E-boat and the skipper gave chase but it turned and ran, and I don't think our captain tried too hard to catch it.

Our patrols went on for several weeks and of course we now knew that we'd taken part in the invasion of Europe. I can't say I did anything heroic but I do admit to being scared rotten, especially when the Germans were shelling and bombing the convoys. Every day was the same; hundreds of ships and landing craft heading for or returning from France.

As is always the case with the services, one day, quite out of the blue, I was told I was being posted elsewhere and had to report to Portsmouth Naval Barracks to get kitted out. We were housed in huge dormitories – 50 sailors to a room – and were issued with tropical clothing, so we knew we were going somewhere warm, or hoped that was the case.

Finally the day came for us to board a troop train, destination unknown. We scraped holes in the blackout paint on the windows and through one of these small cracks I was able to see some familiar landmarks, for example the Tyne Bridge. We stopped in Newcastle for a short while before heading west to Liverpool and right to the docks before boarding the MS Christian Huygens, a Dutch liner that had been transformed into a troop ship.

After two or three days we set sail, to the accompaniment of a Royal Marine Band which, among other tunes, played 'For Those In Peril On The Sea'. We hoped it wasn't an omen, but nevertheless we sang along with great gusto. We set off in a convoy of about 15 ships, including two destroyers. Boredom set in quickly until about three days into the journey, when we were mustered on deck to be told we were going to the Far East and that our first stop would be Cape Town, some four weeks away. From then on it was an uneventful voyage, interrupted only by the destroyers suddenly heading off to the horizon one afternoon and releasing a couple of depth charges. Evidently a submarine had been shadowing us, but we never knew if it had been sunk.

Arriving at Cape Town was a most wonderful event for a kid who only about 12 months previously had never been further than a few miles from home. It seemed the most exotic place on earth; an impression heightened when we were given shore leave and were billeted on a farm that contained the most luxurious bungalow. It was a huge place, populated by servants, and the family couldn't do enough for us. Our first meal was a dinner fit for a King and although it was lavish I didn't enjoy it that much, because I had no idea which piece of cutlery to use. The owner of the farm noticed this and kindly steered us towards his wife, who demonstrated the technique. There were comfortable beds and a swimming pool in the garden – what more could we want? Going back to the ship was like heading to earth with an almighty bump, and unfortunately we never got ashore again. The rest of our time in Cape Town was spent 'vittling ship', which meant taking stores on board and stowing them away.

Our next stop was Sri Lanka, or Ceylon as it was known back then. To pass away the days we gambled and I did very well, winning £26 – more money than I'd ever had in my life. The day before we reached Colombo someone broke into my locker and stole my money belt. I dared not tell anyone, as gambling was an imprisonable offence in the Navy.

So the first month in Ceylon was rather lean, financially speaking, and I had to borrow some rupees from mates until payday came. It was a shame, because the NAAFI was stocked with all sorts of goodies you couldn't get at home; Cadbury's chocolate, tinned and fresh fruit and plentiful supplies of cheap cigarettes. I had my first taste of beer in Colombo with a friend from home, John Cato, and the first sip gave me a lifelong hatred of the stuff. I also had tea with my cousin, Florrie Grey, who was an officer in the WRAC. She took me to the Galle Face Hotel and we were having a lovely time until an RN Lieutenant came over, pointing out that this was an officers' club and that I would have to leave. Despite Florrie's objections that I was her guest, he insisted.

Soon I was drafted to Mandapam in southern India, another shore base, with a wonderful stretch of beach. Our radio office was busy because Mandapam was the major assembly point for an armada of ships that would be attacking the Japanese along the Malacca Straits. However, we still had time to swim in the Indian Ocean, but apart from an open-air cinema there wasn't much to do with our precious spare time. There was a flurry of excitement when it was announced that the Commander South East Asian Forces, Earl Mountbatten, was coming to inspect the camp. The preparations for his visit put us all under great stress because everything seemingly had to be cleaned, painted or polished.

Having been a communications officer, Mountbatten was interested in radio and so he came to our office and thanked us for doing a good job. My only claim to fame in life is that I got to say, 'Good morning, Sir' to a member of the Royal Family and the man who became First Lord of the Admiralty as well as the last Viceroy of India. He was very popular with the servicemen but his wife, Edwina, was not much liked. I don't know how true this is, but it was said that she was responsible for an order making all Naval personnel wear underpants. I believe she was supposed to have seen some startling sights of sailors' nether regions when they were riding rickshaws!

Among those gathered for the attack on the Malacca Straits were several war correspondents, and it was the BBC's man who organised a forces' 'messages home' broadcast. Ten of us were picked out at random from the thousands at Mandapam and I was one of the lucky ones. We had to go to Madras for this and after a very trying, mosquito-ridden night in an RAF camp on the outskirts of the city, we were taken to a BBC studio where we wrote our messages on a form to be read later. Then we were trooped down for the live broadcast. We were all lined up and the announcer said something like, 'Telegraphist Roberts with a message for his mother at 51 Addison Road, West Boldon,' and then I stepped forward and read my message into the microphone.

Perhaps it was mosquito-related, but three weeks after my return to Mandapam I started getting terrible headaches, sweats and shivers, so I went to the sick bay. I was told I had a cold, but during my watch that night I felt truly terrible and reported to the sick bay on my hands and knees. I became delirious, was hospitalised and remained there for ten days in a semi-conscious state. I had been very ill with malaria, and after a further period of hospitalisation I was sent on sick leave to the Nilgiri Hills in southern India for three weeks' rest.

This was one of the most exclusive hill stations in the entire sub-continent and its beauty left me speechless. The trees, wild flowers and even the vegetation were wonderful, not to mention seeing butterflies bigger than a man's hand and birds with plumage beyond description. Our destination, Ootacamund, had a reputation for snobbery but actually it wasn't like that at all. The society ladies living there organised dances, hikes into the forest, swimming in icy mountain pools, picture shows, visits to tea plantations, games of billiards, canteens which sold real cream teas — the pleasures just went on and on. Yet away from these circles it was frowned upon for us to fraternise with these ladies. What a funny world it was back then…

The last two days in the Nilgiri Hills were miserable because President Roosevelt died and everything was closed down as a mark of respect. We were in mourning, but not entirely for the late President; the real misery came from the fact that we could not go to the pictures or have any other entertainment. The journey back to Mandapam was just as wonderful as it had been to the hill station. I recall the smells; the fragrant aroma of burning joss sticks and sandalwood, dank decaying smells from the forest replaced by those of exotic tropical flowers hanging heavy in the still night air. There was the aroma of curry, of course, that came wafting in through the carriage windows whenever a town or village was passed.

Mandapam was a hive of activity when I got back. All kinds of heavy equipment were being loaded on to transports known as Liberty Ships, with tanks and jeeps being directed towards landing craft. It was evident this was going to be a very major assault and we were sending, receiving, encoding and decoding signals night and day. I was on the 0400-0800 morning watch and most of the time we had been getting messages on the Admiralty Broadcast frequencies and keeping in close contact with Mountbatten's HQ in Ceylon. We had to stand by for an 'O' signal, the highest priority (emergency) message. At around 0740 one August morning of 1945 I was sitting with my headphones on, dreaming of having a bacon and egg breakfast and a couple of hours' sleep, when I had to grab my pencil and start taking the longest plain language message I have ever read in my life.

It was the announcement of the Japanese surrender, giving instructions that RN ships were not to engage the enemy unless they fired first. I was yelling to my fellow operators, 'Come and look at this!' and soon there was a knot of officers peering over my shoulder and grabbing each message pad as I completed it. When I eventually came off duty at about 9am I had forgotten all about breakfast and sleep. Everyone in my mess was jumping for joy, slapping each other on the back and sounding like it was us alone who'd won the war. Now, officially, the Second World War was over and we all seemed to think we would be home in a matter of weeks. Had I known that I was doomed to more than another year in the Far East I doubt I would have been that happy.

As peace broke out Mandapam returned to its old sleepy self. Mountbatten was on his way to Singapore to accept the Japanese surrender there, and there were plans for the repatriation of prisoners. Meanwhile, a large group of Wrens came to visit us, along with an ENSA concert party, and the reception the girls got when they arrived by landing craft was enthusiastic, to say the least. As ever, the officers got the pick of the bunch and it was only after two days of their hospitality that the girls were allowed near the other ranks. That didn't go down well, and when our turn came you either had to be very quick or extremely handsome to get a dance or engage them in conversation. Well, some of our crew must have been both, because many of these girls ended up pregnant and some months later I had the dubious duty of taking these unfortunate Wrens back to the UK on the aircraft carrier HMS Formidable.

How did I get aboard that particular ship? Out of the blue I was drafted to her when she was anchored off Mandapam, taking on stores en route for Singapore. So that is where I went, and arrived just in time to see Mountbatten, in immaculate white Naval uniform and lashings of gold braid, go ashore in the Admiral's launch to accept the surrender. We soon followed him after a number of lorries had been unloaded from our ship. When we went ashore there were Japanese everywhere. It was the nearest I'd ever been to them and I wondered why I hated these timid-looking little men kowtowing to all and sundry as they handed in their weapons.

Two sailors were assigned to each covered lorry and mine had a Malay driver. We were told we would be going to Changi jail to pick up a group of Allied prisoners and bring them back to the ship. When we arrived at the jail I realised why I hated the Japanese after all. The POWs were skin and bone, barefoot and so severely malnourished that we were strictly forbidden from offering them chocolate, or food of any kind for that matter. Eating in *quantity could've killed them. All we could offer them were cigarettes. I had never seen people so ill as these prisoners and after four trips to Changi and back, I returned to my accommodation thinking that this had been the most harrowing day of the war for me. Years later my son Gordon was working in London and at his place of work was a caretaker. During a conversation, he mentioned he once knew a sailor on the Formidable called Roberts. Between them, they established that I was the Roberts in question and the caretaker remembered we had become good friends on the voyage to Sydney. There were so many that I do not remember him, but I did recall that all the ex-POWs were given a Formidable pennant as they disembarked. The caretaker subsequently sent this to me and it became a treasured possession.*

Personnel on RN ships are divided into four watches; Red, Green, Blue and Yellow, and when a ship was in harbour two watches were allowed to go ashore at a time. When we arrived in Sydney, Yellow and Blue watches went first, but unfortunately many of these matelots became drunk and caused a lot of trouble with the locals. Consequently all shore leave was cancelled so, having voyaged to the other side of the world, I didn't even get the chance to step on to Australian soil. However, the disappointment was soon overcome when the ship's company were told that we were setting sail for Blighty via Colombo, and we would be demobbed when we reached the UK.

Eventually we anchored off Colombo just long enough to take on the pregnant Wrens from Mandapam. They were strictly segregated and we wouldn't see them again until we reached Portsmouth. Off we went again and when we were anchored in the Red Sea the crew were allowed to swim. Many of the more daring actually dived from the flight deck into the water, but I made my way down to a bulkhead door just above the waterline and very gently lowered myself in. The following day, a Sunday, we were all required to attend morning service and I found it impressive and moving to stand with hundreds of my shipmates while singing the traditional Naval hymn 'Eternal Father Strong To Save.'

A rumour swept the ship that the four aircraft we had on board were to be dumped at sea. I thought of all the pots and pans people back home had handed in to make the planes to fight the war, and here we were about to throw perfectly good aircraft into the sea. Some of the more enterprising lads aboard were not about to let everything go to waste and most of the instruments and all the Perspex was stripped away one night. When this was discovered it was ordered that the looting stop and anyone found with bits of the planes in their possession would be court martialled. A 24-hour guard was put on the aircraft, but the rumour turned out to be true and a few days later a lot of us were ordered to push them over the bow as we steamed astern. The Perspex was soon being fashioned into brooches and lighters for girlfriends back home and as far as I know no one was ever charged with such heinous crimes.

After a period of shore leave in Malta, which was badly damaged by German bombing, we finally arrived in Portsmouth on February 5, 1946, to a very warm welcome from the dockers holding a banner aloft declaring 'Welcome Home to the Forgotten Army'. Seeing there were only a very small number of squaddies aboard, we sailors were a bit miffed. There were loads of mums and dads, wives and kids waving and cheering, and I remember feeling very lonely as there was no one to meet me. This soon passed when I had a night ashore and the next day was taken with other blokes in my demob group to Fort Southwick. This place had been Eisenhower's and Montgomery's invasion HQ for D-Day but was now a demob camp, where we would spend a few days completing the routine for our release from the Royal Navy.

The first meeting we had was a pep talk from a Naval Commander, telling us that we could do no better than to volunteer to continue our Naval careers. Unsurprisingly, this was greeted with a lot of derision from the lads eager to get home. We were informed that we would get 56 days demob leave and as well as our wages for that time we would get a 'demob grant'. After the period of leave we were to report to the Labour Exchange to sign on, then, if we had been employed for a certain time before joining up, we could get our old jobs back. As I'd left the shipyard on medical grounds I could not take advantage of this, but was told there were jobs for radio operators in the Post Office and Coastguard service that I could apply for.

Next we were measured by a man from Burton's the tailors before being shown racks of clothing, from which we could choose a suit, tie, shirts, hat, raincoat, socks and underclothing. We were allowed to keep our Naval uniform, hammock and kit bag but all other equipment had to be handed in. The next day we received an emergency ration card to last until we could apply for civilian issue, plus all our pay and a chit saying how much gratuity would be sent to us at the end of our leave. We also received the all-important rail warrant to get us home. From Portsmouth I took the train to London and then on to Newcastle. By now, the blackout paint had been removed from the carriage windows and I could plot the progress of my journey.

I got a bit of a hero's welcome when I returned to West Boldon, especially from my mam. She hung a 'Welcome Home' banner on our front door and, it being a small village, everyone wanted to know where I'd been and what I'd done.

I was soon picking up where I left off and with my best pal, Roy Moore, was doing the rounds of local dances and picture palaces. Our programme would go something like: Monday – pictures in Sunderland; Tuesday – dancing at Wetheralls; Wednesday – dancing at the Aubrey Leak Hall, West Boldon; Thursday - dancing at Seaburn; Friday - dancing at the Congressional Hall, East Boldon; Saturday – more dancing at the Miners' Hall, Boldon Colliery… and on Sunday we spent a lot of time at St Nicholas Church as Roy was in the choir and I took up serving again. We had at least two services on a Sunday, and after Evensong, dressed in our best bib and tucker and hair slicked back with Brylcreem, we were off out again.

On one of my first visits to the 'Cong' Hall this gorgeous bit of stuff came and buzzed me off during the Ladies Excuse-Me. I don't think the girl I'd been dancing with, Joan Tinling, was very pleased because in Boldon, where there were still loads of soldiers and airmen, a sailor was a rarity and considered to be a bit of a catch. From that moment there was no other girl in the hall and I danced with her just enough to let her not think I was throwing myself at her!

By this time I knew she was called Olive. I asked to take her home and she accepted. We walked up to the post office when she said we would have to go back as she lived down the village. Even when we got back opposite the

Cong, where we had been all night, and next door to the Parish hall, where we sat on a wall, still the penny didn't drop. As I waited for my bus home I fixed up to meet her in a few days' time to go to the pictures, and when my bus was coming up from Blacks Corner I dashed across the road to catch it. I'd just sat down when it suddenly hit me — 'It's that girl with the funny gran!!' I could not get home quick enough to tell my mam that I'd found her again and got a date.

The occasion was for Saturday night flicks in Sunderland and I could hardly wait for the time to pass to meet her again. I know now that I had fallen hook, line and sinker and the only thing that marred our first few weeks' courtship was that she washed her hair on a Friday night. It wasn't long before I took her home to meet mam, and Olive Armstrong became and remained the love of my life.

My brother Bobbie aged about four just before he died of meningitis.

1. Auntie Bella and Uncle Peter with my 'Mam', 'Nell' and me on the stepping stones at Morpeth, the photo was taken by my father. I was aged about three.
2. My 'Mam', me, Uncle Peter and Auntie Bella on the river Wansbeck in 1931.

Grandma Arthur and me. She had come to pick me up after my summer holiday at Auntie Agnes's house. I was about 8 and my 'Mam' had just died.

1. Uncle Peter, Auntie Bella, my 'Mam' and me. The photo was posed by my dad.
2. My cousin Elsie, my Dad and me in the poppy fields at Mitford.

This is a picture of my dad – I had this folded in a frame for a long time and is one of the few pictures I have of him.

1. Ron's 'Mam' 'Jane' (centre) taken at the turn of the 19th to 20th century. She was manageress of the Harry Taylor shop. This photo was taken at Christmas and they had decorated the window with cotton wool as pretend snow.
2. This is Ron's father, Moses Roberts, second from the left with his friends.

1. Moses Roberts.

2. Ron's brother William (Bill) Roberts, taken 16th January 1920 on his first day down the pit at Bolden Colliery.

3. Ron's elder brothers.

4. Ron on the knee of an 'Uncle' (middle) with his father Moses on the far left – always with his flat cap!

1. Three Roberts brothers, Bill, Fred and Arthur.
2. Ron's 'Mam' with Ron on her knee soon after he had been born, in the back (right) his sister Edna.
3. Ron (right) and a cousin when they were 18 months old.
4. Ron as a child (left front) with his family. Taken 19th June 1927, a day before his second birthday.

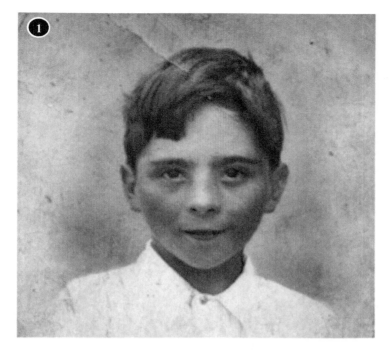

1. Ron's first school photo aged 6.
2. Ron with his sister Edna and 'Mam' Jane.

1 and 3. Ron when he had joined the RAF after his training in the navy.

2. Ron when he first joined the Navy before he joined a ship, note the wireless badge on his arm, he was very proud of this!

4. Ron when he was in the Air Training Corp before he joined up, it was where he first learnt semaphore and morse code.

5.. Ron when he was at his training ship.

6.. Ron in his overseas uniform and this is exactly how I remember him when I first saw him.

Ron on service in Mandapam in Ceylon in 1947.

1 and 2. These pictures were taken before we got married, Ron was going to Brora and wanted a photo of me to take with him.

3. Ron's 'Mam' Jane, this photo was taken at her front door by a travelling photographer. They used to go around taking photos and then force you to buy their pictures.

4. Ron and me on my 21st birthday in March 1949, my gran bought the dress for me as a birthday present and we told her that we were going to get married. She said no... but gave in, in the end.

Our wedding photo and the wedding cake. Made by our local Coop with eggs that Ron brought from Brora.

Our wedding day and reception in the parish hall 27th August 1949.

1. Wedding photo with my cousin Hilary (Elsie's daughter) – my little bridesmaid, she would not leave me alone on the day.
2. Ron and me in Blackpool for our honeymoon.
3. Me in the garden taken by Ron.
4. Me with the handbag that I made! Outside my grandma's cottage at 18 Front Street going to Church for Good Friday prayers.
5. Ron and me with Sally our first dog.

1. Ron in his demob coat.
2. Ron and me with Colin and Sally our dog. I was pregnant with Gordon.
3. Ron at his lodgings in Brora before we got married.
4. Ron and me with Colin, Gordon and Sally in Beverley.

1. Colin and Gordon making sandcastles on the beach at Hastings.
2. Ron and Gordon with a stray dog we 'adopted' which unfortunately bit someone and had to be put to sleep!
3. Gordon on Christmas morning in 1960 dressed in his Christmas presents – a cowboy's outfit! Taken in Appledore.
4. Colin with his Christmas present – roller skates in Appledore.
5. Me with Nigel soon after he was born in 1961.
6. My cousin Pat and me in 1960.

1 and 2. Gordon and Colin at the funfair in Margate.
3. Gordon on the beach at Margate.
4. Ron's cousin Margaret Roberts and me on the beach at Margate – I was expecting Nigel.
5. Ron and a newly-born Nigel in February 1961.
6. Gordon on his trike at Appledore.

1. Gordon and Nigel at the cubs in Singapore about 1964, Gordon was taking part in a fancy-dress competition.
2. Nigel jumping into the pool at Singapore Swimming Club.
3. Nigel varnishing a ratan basket with me watching - at our house in Siglap Avenue, Singapore.
4. Suckling pigs being roasted outside our house in Singapore.
5. Me standing outside the Sri Thendayuthapani Hindu Temple in Singapore.
6. Nigel sitting on Ron on the Blakang Mati island in Singapore.

1. Colin, Gordon and Ron at the fishing ponds in Singapore.
2.. Colin posing by the sea!
3. Nigel and Sandra (the daughter of my cousin Margaret).
4. Johnnie Hamill (Uncle Johnnie) with Gordon and Nigel at the Singapore Swimming Club.
5. David Watson (my cousin Margaret's husband) and me taking photos of the photographer.
6. David, Ron, my cousin Margaret, Nigel and Sandra, Colin and Gordon.

CHAPTER 8 – WEDDING BELLS

So now you know what Ron did in the war, and how we were reunited at the dance. And yes, I agreed to go with him to the pictures and we had a lovely evening, despite my gran's mutterings about him. She knew his mother and didn't like her much, even though she seemed perfectly fine to me when we eventually met.

The problem was that gran was keen for me to meet a 'professional' man. A junior doctor, perhaps, or a trainee solicitor. Someone with prospects, who could lift me out of East Boldon and give me the kind of life she never had… one in which money wasn't always an issue. Looking back, I understand her logic. She'd struggled her entire life and she didn't want the same for me. But I was young and carefree and adventurous. What I wanted, and what she wanted for me, were two different things then.

Besides, I liked Ron. We suited each other – we both liked dancing, going to the pictures and having fun. It's true that he was just out of the Navy, and not likely to go back to the shipyard, and so what prospects he had were a bit of a mystery at that stage.

Even so, he was an enthusiastic young man and I had no worries about him finding something sooner or later.

There was also the slight problem about Jimmy Swan, the Navy lad from Glasgow that I'd been seeing. As I mentioned, he'd been sent down to Portsmouth to be demobbed and I felt obliged to tell Ron that I did have a boyfriend who'd said he'd be back for me. But as the days passed and he neither showed up nor wrote to me, I became increasingly sceptical that I'd ever see him again. Ron felt the same. "I think he's done a runner," he said, "and gone home to Glasgow." I was a bit upset, but not that much. And he never did turn up, so Ron seemed to have been right.

Ron and I started seeing more and more of each other. He applied to the Post Office for the job of Radio Operator, but in the meantime he took a job as a tea salesman with the Home and Country Tea Company. He was meant to have a driving licence in order to drive the Trojan van he would be given as part of the job, but he didn't have one. However, just the fact that he agreed to take lessons seemed to satisfy his prospective boss and he was offered the position. The wage was £4 a week plus commission but I don't think he ever earned any commission – he was too busy giving me lifts to and from work! My boss was quite surprised to see a man in a dustcoat collect me at lunchtime, and a few questions were asked of Ron, but I never minded that.

I had the same kind of questioning from my gran. "Why are you going with him?" she'd say. "All he does is drive a van." But we were happy together and I enjoyed travelling in the Trojan, laughing at Ron's mishaps and failure to persuade housewives all over the area to buy his tea, biscuits, sugar and tinned foods. I did invite Ron back to our home but gran made it clear she didn't like him and that was awkward, to say the least. There were times that gran wouldn't speak to me and somehow I was made to feel as though I were a troublemaker. I always had cousin Elsie to back me up and defend me but gran tried hard to get the rest of the family on her side, and that led to increased tension between us. Gran would claim that my relationship with Ron was causing her heartache and making her ill. All I could do was bite my lip, bide my time and hold on to the fact that at 21 I would be able to leave the house as a married woman – because after about six months' courting, Ron asked me to marry him.

Now, I was still only 18 and at that age I still needed permission from a parent or guardian to get married. As I didn't have parents, my next of kin was gran – and she was highly unlikely to allow me to become a teenage bride by marrying Ron. I look back now and see that, aside from the fact she wanted me to marry a professional man, she was just being protective over me. I could barely fry an egg, never mind give up work (which newly married women had to do then, of course) and become a full-time housewife. She was right not to grant me permission, even though it was an intense source of frustration at the time.

Eventually, Ron was called away to Post Office HQ in London for the radio operator's interview. The circumstances of this appointment all seemed a bit secretive and at the time we were due to go on holiday to Ron's sister in Leeds. We managed to have a nice couple of days, although Ron was preoccupied with brushing up on his Morse, which he hadn't kept up with since he left the Navy. I stayed in Leeds while he went to London, where he faced a tough interview from a panel of people who wanted to know if he or any of his family had been communists. He came back two days later, telling us that he'd also been asked whether he was prepared to sign the Official Secrets Act. He was, and so we enjoyed the rest of our time in Leeds and waited to see what would turn up.

A week or so after we arrived home Ron received the news that he'd been accepted, and would be starting his radio operator's training at the Post Office Wireless Training College at Bletchley Park, Buckinghamshire – the place where the Nazi Enigma Code was broken, helping to turn the tide of war against them. In Ron's own words, here's some of what happened during those months:

I eventually got my instructions to report to Bletchley Park at 9am on Monday, and armed with my free rail warrant I set off to catch the overnight train from Newcastle to London, escorted to the railway station by my mam and Olive. I would have much rather left mam at home because my goodbyes to Olive had to be restricted to a polite peck on the cheek with mother in attendance.

Changing trains in London I caught my connection for Bletchley at 4am for the 40-minute trip. I must have gone off into a sound sleep because the next thing I knew was a cleaner waking me up and telling me we were in a siding at Bletchley and it was 7.30am. I was instructed to walk with care along the line back to the station and it would be no good to rush up to the Park as they would not let me in until 8.30am. Just outside the station there was a railwaymen's club where I could purchase breakfast much more cheaply than in the station buffet. I trudged back along the line carrying my old battered Navy suitcase and found the club to enjoy a jolly good breakfast for about ninepence old money. As we got subsistence to buy food while on the training course this information about the railwaymen's club was to save me a lot of money over the seven months I spent at the Post Office Wireless Training College.

Reporting to block D lower training school at nine 'o'clock I met up with most of the fellows who had been on the initial interview with me. We were allocated accommodation, two to a room, in very comfortable quarters. My roommate was Ron Watson and I suppose that was my nearest brush with fame in my whole career as Ron went on to become a Principal Station Officer and that was about as high as one could get in the Radio Grade. Ron and I remained good friends over the years, though our paths rarely crossed.

Our first two weeks at the park were a great 'swan' as we were on what was called an induction course, spending a lot of time filling in forms which seemed mainly aimed at finding out our own and immediate family's political leanings. We soon found out that the Post Office were not very keen on Communists or anyone that had leanings to the left. Even expressing sympathy with the Labour Party was frowned on. Being civil servants, we were told we should be non-political and never join a political party, although it was made quite clear that it would be to our advantage to vote in Tory elections. This was not easy for a young lad brought up in a mining village.

Lots of time was spent on learning Civil Service jargon and very importantly how to fill in subsistence claims, and a clever way of cooking the books by knowing how to fill in the forms correctly to get everything you were entitled to. At the beginning of the third week we were introduced to the Bottom School radio course and soon found out that it was not going to be such a 'swan' after all. We were required to pass weekly Morse tests at a given speed throughout the eight-week course and learned that Friday was 'chop day'. That meant that if you did not pass two consecutive Morse tests at the given speed on the Friday, you would be escorted to the Officer-in-Charge's office, given a week's wages and your cards then be shown the door, never to return.

Unfortunately quite a number of excellent Radio Operators suffered this fate because they suffered from examination nerves. I suppose I was lucky that I was not bright enough to realise that I should be worried and so survived, to the point where I was reading 26 wpm plain language, 28 wpm five letter code and 30 wpm cypher or five-figure group code. During this time we were also taught touch typing and teleprinter operating that had to be learned to a certain degree of expertise to escape the Friday Chop. Looking back now I think that must have been very stressful but somehow I thoroughly enjoyed it and sailed through the eight weeks without a blemish.

Now we were through to the Upper School, and on our first Monday we were all assembled into a large lecture room and told that if we wanted to continue working for the PO we would be required to sign the Official Secrets Act. As the course progressed we would have to be willing to be indoctrinated to higher and higher degrees of security clearance, and for the first time we were informed that our work would not be normal radio communications but intercept work - which did not mean a thing to any of us - but it was explained that we would be charged with finding transmissions that the originators did not really want us to read. They also told us that from this day forward we were never to write or type even a letter we were not absolutely sure was right, as breaking codes was difficult enough without introducing spurious figures or letters. We were still not told who we would be intercepting or why, but I admit there was quite a buzz of excitement at the suggestion that this might be spying.

Up to now, being at Bletchley Park had been a piece of cake but now we were breaking new ground, the leisurely life of finishing work at 5pm and sprucing up to go to dances at the Old Hall, visits to the cinema and the occasional adventurous trip to see a show in London all went out of the window. Our days were spent taking copious notes which all had to be rewritten, studied and absorbed after finishing work, and this meant burning a lot of the midnight oil. Not only had we to learn about the communications methods of our perceived enemies, but a lot of attention was given to the diplomatic links of friendly nations such as France and the USA. Much to our surprise, we would also be keeping a sharp eye on our own military and diplomatic communications. Over the years the reason for this type of activity gradually made some sense but for a long time I felt I had got myself mixed up in the 'dirty tricks brigade'.

The daily routine was much the same throughout our time in the Upper School. The mornings would be taken up with live radio interception work and the afternoons spent in the lecture rooms, with an instructor pumping us full of information about civil, military and diplomatic communication methods, particularly those of Russia, Germany, Poland, China, Japan, and all the places that eventually became known as the countries behind the Iron Curtain. Even the Vatican came under our surveillance and I learned over the years not to be too surprised at what those Popes got up to. The Vatican went to extraordinary lengths to protect known Nazi war criminals who professed they were also Catholic.

When the course was coming to a close we were shown a list of intercept stations around Britain and asked to make a first and second choice of where we would like to be posted. At this stage I should point out that we had already signed a contract agreeing to accept postings anywhere in the world, and to refuse meant almost certain dismissal. The nearest station to home was

Scarborough, and as my only ambition was to be as near to Olive as possible, I chose there, saying that I had no other choice. The Station Officer, Mr Friar, was a chap with the gift of the gab and on chop day he could call someone into his office and make them feel they were being promoted while he was telling them they were fired. He called me into his office and told me I had no chance of getting to Scarborough but if I would agree to go to Brora (in Scotland) on a temporary posting for about eight weeks he would make sure I would get to Cupar, which was the nearest station to Newcastle. I left that office feeling I had been given a bonus, having agreed to go to Brora.

Ron and I kept in contact by letter and telephone, though it was never very easy to arrange a phone call when both of us were using phone boxes. He had a week's leave before his posting to Brora and when that was finished, off he went, and life carried on in the usual way of letters and the occasional phone call.

When the summer holidays came around Ron invited me up to Brora for a week. After a train journey that seemed to last forever, I got off the train to be met by a porter who seemed to know my name and informed me that I would be staying with Mrs McGregor, Ron's landlady, as she had another spare room. It seemed to me that everyone knew everything about me before I'd even arrived and I found that just a bit weird. Anyway, we would borrow a couple of bicycles and explore the countryside around Brora, or just visit the beach for a picnic because the weather was so good. One of the reasons for visiting was to see whether I could live up in that area as a married woman. I'm afraid that on this occasion I said 'no'; it was a long way from everywhere and it seemed very insular to me. So Ron and I agreed that we wouldn't get married until he'd been posted somewhere more suitable.

Here is a bit more from Ron about the work he did in Brora:

On our arrival I reported to our new supervisor, resplendent behind his control desk. He pushed an upturned trilby hat towards me with bits of screwed up paper in and told me to pick one. I got No.1 and the supervisor said, 'Right laddie, grab yourself a bit of slip and bed down behind the radio racks and we will call you when we want you.'

I lay there, listening to the rattle of undulators and printers and wondering what I had come to. Well, as time passed I went to sleep and unfortunately was forgotten. I was wakened by the day watchman telling me it was about time I went home, and so ended my first working night in the employ of the Post Office Wireless Service.

The following day I was on night shift again and soon found out that the work was not going to be one long bed of slip. To the uninitiated, 'slip' is paper about a quarter of an inch wide and hundreds of yards long, used for recording high-speed Morse via an undulator. It made very good bedding too. At Brora, our cover was Russian military and commercial broadcasts from many different countries. You might wonder why we were intercepting commercial activity. Well, when I was in training it had all been explained. Lots of diplomatic traffic was sent on the commercial networks and sometimes those messages provided the piece of the jigsaw that led to breaking codes. The commercial stuff was of interest because, for example, machine tools to be shipped to a destination we were interested in could tell us that they may be manufacturing arms or ammunition in that particular area. Even a change in the amount of food ordered for a garrison might lead us to finding out that a regiment was being deployed.

As far as our marriage and a new posting was concerned Ron was as good as his word and he asked his station commander whether he could have the posting to either Scarborough or Cupar as soon as possible – otherwise he would go home and not come back. That was quite bold of him, and in fact he did purchase the ticket because when his next leave came up, he still hadn't been posted. He came home, and we went to the usual dances, films and choir practice while Ron tried not to worry about what might happen next. Anyway, four days before his leave was due to end he received a letter from HQ telling him his move to Hawklaw was confirmed and we were both very relieved indeed. Hawklaw was a GCHQ station in Cupar, Fife, primarily engaged in intercepting messages from the Eastern Bloc; about 100 people worked there. (It was closed in 1988.) So off he went to Fife, where he found accommodation with a Mrs Kirk.

Ron had done the right thing by me, and now it was time for me to return the favour by accepting his proposal of marriage and fixing a date for the wedding, which was to be August 27, 1949, at St George's Church, East Boldon. By then I would have reached 21 and no longer needed my gran's permission, though she was still making life difficult for me. Her attitude towards Ron and his mother (whom she really disapproved of now, because she'd married again after the war) hadn't changed and some days she was going to the wedding, other days not.

By this time I'd changed jobs. When the war ended those boys who'd worked at MacKenzie and Co before joining up were offered their jobs back. So a lot of us girls found ourselves redundant. The irony was that, having been away and experienced all sorts of adventures, the returning men weren't so bothered about becoming 'office boys' again. And who could blame them? The war had changed everything and people didn't automatically do as they were told any more.

I didn't mind so much about losing my job because I knew so many people in the John Street area, and in fact a friend recommended me for a job in a firm of accountants. I didn't know much about figures but I went along for an interview anyway and got a job as one of the head typists, where I stayed until I got married.

We started making preparations for the wedding. I went to the Fenwick's department store in Newcastle and bought myself some material which I had made up into a lovely white suit, complete with matching hat. For the first time I had my own money because grandma said I could keep all my wages for the six weeks leading up to the wedding. Previously, I'd always handed my wage packet to her and she'd given me an allowance from it.

I didn't want to wear a long white dress because I had no father to give me away and somehow it didn't feel right. However, Uncle Peter volunteered to take on that duty so at least I wouldn't be on my own. I wanted a pair of wedge shoes, the height of fashion in 1949, and Fenwick's had to send away to America for the precise pair I was after. My bridesmaid was to be my cousin Norrie, who was very tomboyish and looked incredibly uncomfortable in her bridesmaid's dress, bless her.

The vicar who married us, the Rev Henderson, had us round before the wedding to give a pep talk about marriage. We were a bit shocked to hear him tell us that Christian marriage was for the creation of children and that we should do nothing to stop this from happening. I'm not sure we really knew what he was on about, and were surprised that he should be talking this way to a yet-unmarried couple. What innocent days they were!

On the day of the wedding itself there seemed to be so many people crowding into grandma's house (she had finally consented to attend the ceremony, despite last-minute mutterings and grumblings) that someone even hung their coat over my wedding suit. I was due to meet cousin Elsie at the Parish Hall so that we could set up all the tables and chairs for the reception. However, she didn't turn up so I was forced to get help from a poor old man just passing by. I wasn't allowed to use the hall's china because it was the property of the Mothers' Union, and obviously I didn't have a mother. My gran stuck up for me on that one but they were adamant, so we had to beg, borrow and steal whatever we could so at least we had plates, cups and saucers.

When I came back, the house was still crowded. Our neighbour, Mrs Gibson, popped in and straight away saw the chaos. "Come into us," she whispered to me, and so I scooped up my things and followed. It was a very good offer because she filled her tin bath with hot water, placed it in her bedroom and let me get on beautifying myself in peace and quiet.

Meanwhile, over in West Boldon, Ron was trying on the suit that he'd paid for but not chosen. It was jet black, a colour much better suited to a funeral, and it had been picked by his mother and his Aunt Alice, who both insisted on this particular colour. I'm glad I didn't know beforehand because when I saw it I could've died on the spot. Aunt Alice told him that it wasn't too late to change his mind (about the wedding, not the suit!) and when he refused her advice she offered him a glass of whisky, which he also refused because in those days he didn't drink.

Finally, everyone cleared out of my house, leaving just me, my gran and Uncle Peter. The wedding car arrived, which was part of a taxi firm being run by a group of local lads who'd returned from the war. Ron and I knew them all, and they assured us that they'd decorate the car with ribbons and be there on time. Well, they were very prompt for me, even though the church was only at the bottom of the street, but less so for Ron because when I arrived at the church the Rev Henderson came down the path and said the groom hadn't yet arrived. I told him it was all arranged and that Ron was due to be picked up. Of course, the lads running the taxi firm had forgotten. So we had to come back to the house while a car was dispatched to collect Ron and his mother.

Eventually, after all the kerfuffle, the wedding went well and even my gran, who had bought a new hat, grudgingly seemed to enjoy the day, though she had little to say to Ron's mother. Photographs were taken, the food was eaten and we all enjoyed a good bit of dancing before it was time to leave for our honeymoon – destination Blackpool. As we were leaving, I went up to my gran expecting a hug and a kiss but instead she just stuck out her hand for me to shake. She was never a person to show much affection, as she'd been shown very little herself when she was a child. I think she must've been sorry that I was leaving her, and in her own way was glad for Ron and me, but just couldn't allow herself to show it without losing face. For me, I was more than ready to leave. Ron and I had waited a long time for this moment and we just wanted to be free at last.

A taxi, tied up with ribbons and trailing old shoes, took us to the Haymarket in Newcastle, from where we caught a bus east to the Lancashire coast. The bus broke down on the way and we were delayed for three hours before we finally made it to the guest house in Hornby Road. Ron had been billeted here in the war and had enjoyed the place, but by this time it had gone downhill and Ron was very disappointed. The room was very small and the landlady nowhere near as friendly as Ron had remembered her during the war, but nevertheless we made the best of it.

Blackpool was a mecca then and we had lots of fun. We went dancing in the Winter Gardens and the Tower Ballroom, we strolled along the prom and roller-skated on the pier. We also fitted in a few shows, including one by Irish tenor Joseph Locke, along with the Jewell and Warris show with Mr and Mrs Andrews and their young daughter Julie. Yes, THE Julie Andrews! We saw the first regional performance of 'Annie Get Your Gun' and by the time we'd seen this and done that, we were quite spent up. So much so that on our final day we counted out what money we had left, and it came to the sum total of sixpence. So Ron bought two Mars Bars and we sat on the bus back to the North East, eating our chocolate and as happy as could be. And in any case we weren't so worried because Ron knew his pay would be waiting at his mother's house. When we arrived there we found to our delight that he'd had a pay rise which had been backdated, so instead of the expected £4 15s he received something in the region of £20. And we felt rich beyond our wildest dreams!

The following day we packed our things, said our farewells and headed to Newcastle train station to begin our married life in Cupar. We would be lodging with Mrs Kirk, Ron's landlady, who had set us up in a two-roomed flat in the basement of her house. This was a tenement building and the flat was very basic indeed; no kitchen and no bath, except for a tin one kept in the cellar. The toilet was also in the cellar, along with the hot water boiler which had to be filled every time you needed warm water.

Still, it was our first home and we were quite proud of it. That changed when I met Mrs Kirk. She forewent any kind of warm welcome to let me know of my duties as her tenant. I would have to scrub the stone steps and Pumice-stone them white every Friday. The wooden steps also had to be scrubbed then covered with newspaper to keep them clean for the Sabbath, when the newspaper would be removed to show them off in all their glory. On wash day I was expected to help Mrs Kirk by filling the boiler with water and lighting the fire underneath so the water would be hot for when she was ready to wash her clothes. In all honesty, while at home with my gran, I'd not been expected to do much more than wash the dishes, so I was totally unprepared for this onslaught of domestic duties. I had to take on these duties, but they only came round once a week for the washing and once a week for the steps, so I had to fill my time at the Church. I joined the Mothers' Union (even though I was not a mother), I took cookery courses in the town, and in this way I got to meet people and make new friends.

Being churchgoers, we joined the Episcopalian Church and the vicar of our local church in Cupar took us under his wing, to the extent that he asked me if I was interested in finding a job locally. I wasn't quite sure that I was, but Ron was quick to say that it might do me good to get out of the house. There didn't seem to be any room to argue so he went away and arranged an interview in the local Procurator Fiscal's office for a secretarial job.

I was interviewed, got the job and started work soon after. But as I quickly found out, 'work' didn't mean work at all, for there seemed to be very little for me to actually do. I thought my domestic situation was old-fashioned, but this was even worse. The people were very nice, but they were dour, and it seemed that a job had been created for me on the orders of the vicar. I would look out of the window into the busy offices across the street and wish I was among the girls I could see in those buildings, gossiping and joking as they typed away. I felt useless; so useless that I would take weeks at a time off in the hope they would sack me. But they didn't. Instead, they considered that I was just getting used to married life and being in a new place, and every Friday without question they'd send round my pay. Whenever I went back in, there was still nothing to do, and they'd just say that I could go home early.

Life seemed to be plodding at this dull place when two things happened that would change everything once again. The first was that Mrs Kirk gave us notice to quit, as her daughter's husband was moving back to Cupar and needed the flat. The second piece of news, which was far better than the first, was that I was pregnant.

CHAPTER 9 – LISTENING IN

Before carrying on with the narrative, at this point I'm going to let Ron tell you a little about what he was doing in Scotland. For obvious reasons he couldn't and didn't talk much about his work (he'd signed the Official Secrets Act, after all) but his narrative contains a few insights into his daily life. He started out with the Post Office Wireless Service but after a time this became the famed GCHQ, which of course is still going strong today. The extracts below are more about his days in Brora, and also his involvement in the union:

I would have a rest day before starting out on a new round of shifts which were 8am-2pm (days), 2pm-10pm (evenings) and 10pm-8am (nights). The days and nights shift was a particularly tough one because you were out of bed early for the morning shift, then back to the digs for a meal and a kip between 2pm-10pm, then back to work for a ten-hour shift. This meant we worked 16 hours out of 24 and, would you believe it, it was not unusual to be scheduled for overtime, which meant you had to report for work at 6pm. So you see – we were some kind of supermen working 20 out of 24 hours a day!

Overtime was compulsory so it had to be done, at least until someone discovered that if you went sick on scheduled overtime you still got paid that overtime. This went on for many years until the department cottoned on to the fact that people only seemed to be ill when they were down for overtime, so it was decided to make it voluntary.

When I came to Cupar I became quite a militant member of staff. We had no union and could only negotiate through a committee made up of members of the official side and the staff side. I can't for the life of me recall the official title of this, but it was a Civil Service-wide organisation and if it was impossible to agree a matter locally, disputes could be passed to the national committee. As I've mentioned, the staff were divided into watches covering a 24-hour day, plus a number of day staff comprising radio operators, radio mechanics, traffic handlers, secretaries, wages clerks, cleaners, drivers, etc. Each watch and the day staff had a representative on this committee and eventually I got myself elected as watch rep.

The chairman of the staff side was a chap called Jim Brodie. He was an ex-Sergeant Major from the Royal Corps of Signals and quite a bit older than the average radio officer. I suppose because of his past experiences he was a wonderful barrack-room lawyer and much respected by staff and the official side. He and I became very good friends and co-conspirators working to improve conditions and pay for us all.

It did not take us long to realise that the way we were organised we were flogging a dead horse, so we set about with staff side members from other stations to form a proper trade union. Much to our surprise (and the official side's too) we got strong support and formed an association called The Civil Servants' Radio Officers' Association (CSROA) headed up by our first president, Arthur Coombs, who got the job mainly because he worked at HQ. There were no paid officers and the official side took very little notice of us. There was no doubt we were poorly paid and as I've described, the shift systems were very anti-social. We tried to put this right but we only nibbled at the edges and had very little success.

Leave was another problem. We inherited a seniority system from the Post Office which meant the oldies who came from that organisation got first go at the leave chart. We younger ones never got a chance of having Christmas or New Year off, and those with school-age children found it near-impossible to get holidays at the same time as their kids. That was a thorn in our side for many years but eventually we got it sorted out by adopting a system where all the names went into a hat and you got the choice in the order the names were picked out. This system seemed fairer but even that had to be modified a few years later when we found some people seemed to be luckier than others. So if you were first out one year you were automatically assigned last pick for the following year.

The CSROA had been going on for a few years when another organisation, The Association of Government Radio Officers (AGSRO) was set up in opposition. Its main achievement was to split the camp into two warring factions, fighting each other for members, so some of us decided that the best thing for us would be to become a branch in a bigger union. So eventually the Department recognised the Civil Service Union (Radio Officers' Section) as the official representative of the radio staff. Jim Brodie became chairman and secretary of the branch and I was appointed treasurer.

Now, back to news from the domestic front! We were a bit worried about where we might go, especially with me being pregnant, but luckily we spotted an advert in the paper placed by a Baptist Minister offering accommodation to a young couple willing to do housekeeping for him. Well, we jumped at that chance and soon we were living at the Manse, in much better accommodation than we'd experienced at Mrs Kirk's, and to cap it all we had our very own dog, a Springer Spaniel we called Sally. She was very special to us, and looked such an aristocrat that we used to peep round the door and watch her while she was asleep, hardly believing that she was ours.

Just before we moved into the Manse, Ron had a warning from someone at work that the minister was a bit of a villain. We didn't believe this, of course, but after a while we found out the truth. We were living there rent-free in return for doing some household chores and the food shopping. At first, the minister was charming, though we found his demands for chores a bit much. Then there was the food bill. We were expected to pay for it all and he put absolutely everything on there, even his cigarettes. We complained, but we were told we'd have to either pay up or leave.

From there, things turned nasty. We tried to eke out a living by collecting firewood from the nearby forest or buy spent fuel from the local gasworks but the bill was becoming large and it was a very stressful time. Eventually we told him we were leaving, and, as it happened, I really wasn't feeling very well with the pregnancy, so I decided to go back to East Boldon while Ron looked for somewhere new for us to live.

I think I may also have been a bit homesick. It was a different world up there; dour, and nowhere near as friendly as my home town. I'd never been away from home before and had found it hard to get used to many new ways. That said, it wasn't at all easy getting used to living with my gran again but Ron assured me he would find somewhere else quickly, and every day I waited for the letter telling me I could return to Scotland.

One weekend I went to visit my Aunt Eadie in Durham. You'll remember that she was the one who adopted my sister Edith, whom I was only to refer to as a cousin. By now, Edith was quite the beauty, tall and willowy, and we got on ever so well. We took a lot of walks around the city with the dog and I remember her saying to me, "It's funny, Olive, but nobody ever talks about your mother…" I was very shocked but all I could reply was, "No, they don't, do they?" And our birth mother was never referred to again. As we will find out later, Edith never did know who her real mother was but I think she had her suspicions, and perhaps she was testing the waters during that walk.

Despite that, I was enjoying myself in Durham when I started to feel pains in my stomach. I should've listened to my body and stayed in Durham but I decided to go back to East Boldon where I felt more at home. I came home on the bus and felt worse with each mile that passed. When I got off, the dog was pulling the lead so much that when I reached my gran's I just collapsed in the chair – and already I was beginning to lose the baby. In her wisdom, gran decided I hadn't been pregnant after all and was just having a heavy period. She confined me to bed and refused to call the doctor. By 2am the following day I was still bleeding heavily and although I begged, gran would not fetch Uncle Peter from next door.

Finally, after I spent ages shouting for Uncle Peter through the wall, he came round, saw the terrible situation unfolding and immediately phoned for the doctor. He and an ambulance arrived at 6am and I was rushed into hospital, where anything that was left of my pregnancy was surgically removed. I regained consciousness in the ward and by then it was visiting time. I waited for someone to tell me what had happened, and whether they'd sent word to Ron, but no one came. The next morning my cousin Elsie had a need to go to the doctor's surgery and she only found out what had happened when he asked her how I was getting on. So she rushed round to Ron's mum's house – and she'd heard nothing either. Finally, gran admitted what had happened and cousin Elsie got in touch with Ron to summon him home.

Ron was furious that he hadn't been told. Later on, he said that the train journey from Cupar to Boldon was the longest of his life because he'd no idea of how I was, or even if I was still alive. When he arrived at gran's he was told that I'd had 'a show' in the night. He'd no idea what a 'show' was, and was too afraid to ask gran. So he came straight to the hospital, where I told him the bad news. It was very strange indeed not to have had any visitors up until that point, even though gran, Auntie Bella and Uncle Peter had all been present when I was losing the baby.

Anyway, after Ron arrived I started to feel a bit better and eventually went back to my gran's while I waited for him to find us a new place. He did this, renting a small room in Short Lane, Cupar. I wasn't much impressed when I got there as it was in a poor state and the area of town wasn't great. The landlady shared the kitchen with us and disclosed that her husband was in prison.

I was nervous about this, as I'd never known anyone who'd been to jail, but when he was released he wasn't the brute I'd imagined – in fact, he was a small, insignificant man. I've no idea what he'd done, and I'm glad I never found out!

To get away from the shabbiness of the room I found a secretarial job with the Ministry of Food (Potato Division). This sounds quite comic now but it was a serious matter – rationing was still in force and there were official Inspectors of potatoes who would visit farms across Scotland making sure that farmers were growing their quota of potatoes. Many of them said they were when they weren't, and therefore had to be inspected.

There was a much better atmosphere in this job than there had been in the Procurator Fiscal's office and I was just settling down to the work when I found myself pregnant again. Ron and I agreed that we didn't want to bring a new baby back to the room in Short Lane so once again we were on the hunt for a new place to live. As luck would have it, one of the men at the Ministry of Food, a Mr Marshall, said he had a cottage on his estate and he and his wife were prepared to let us live in it rent-free. Mr Marshall's wife was from the North East – Houghton-le-Spring – and they took to us as if we were related. They'd lost a lot of money at the start of the Depression but they obviously weren't short of a penny or two. The problem was that the cottage was in Gillingshill, out in the countryside, and Ron wasn't sure how he'd get to work. This was solved when he decided to buy himself a BSA Bantam motorbike and although we had no money we somehow purchased it on the never-never!

These next few paragraphs are how Ron remembers this period:

Our time at Gillingshill was very happy, despite being as poor as church mice. I got involved with the Pittenweem Episcopalian Church and took up serving again. We became very friendly with the Rector and through him got ourselves involved in a lot of social activities. As he was a bachelor he became a regular visitor to our home for meals and he returned the favour by having us to dine at the Rectory. He was a jolly good cook and we had some great nights out there.

He reckoned the building, which was an old priory, was haunted and he used to delight in showing us the old priest-holes and where the ghost would appear. One night I was visiting him when we heard a tapping at the window and I looked up and near died on the spot. There was a hooded face peering in! I must have looked ashen because he said, "It's alright, it's just the district nurse who pops in about this time to tell me how her patients are." I can tell you he repeated that story at every opportunity when I was around.

Of course, without my trusty BSA Bantam none of this socialising would have been possible because Gillingshill was a long way from towns for shopping or places of entertainment. The bike enabled Olive and me to have the occasional visit to the cinema, visit friends in Cupar and its surrounding villages, and on rare occasions get as far afield as Dundee, which was our nearest big town.

This time, my pregnancy progressed very well. Mrs Marshall was very kind to me and even let me sleep in one of the huge bedrooms 'up at the big house' when Ron was on nights. Little did she know that I was more frightened than I was on my own in the cottage. We regularly had visitors from Boldon, including Auntie Bella, Uncle Peter, cousin Elsie and her husband Denis (the latter pair coming for their honeymoon). I did have a few problems with my blood pressure and water retention and as there were no buses I used to attend the clinics miles away on the back of Ron's bike. I was even transported to the maternity hospital on it, and it was there on August 10, 1951, that I gave birth to a baby boy, whom we would call Colin. In those days the baby was taken away from you straight away and put in the nursery, while you were given all the attention. On the third day, when the milk came through, the baby was handed back and so began the lifelong job of being a mother. I was in the hospital for a month – two weeks before Colin was born and two weeks after.

It's incredible to think now that so much time could be devoted to a new mother.

We were still churchgoers and so naturally we wanted Colin to be christened. The local vicar, who was a lovely man, would've happily done it but we felt we'd like the christening to take place at St George's church in East Boldon, where we'd been married. So the next time we visited the area we went to see the Rev Henderson, who'd married us, confident there would be no problem. Unfortunately he wasn't having any of it. "Oh, I don't think so," he said dismissively. "I don't need to christen this baby. It should be christened where you are now living."

Ron argued that we were now in Scotland, and that it would be very hard for his mother and my grandmother to attend the event. But his pleas fell on deaf ears and the Rev Henderson shooed us away. We were so upset, particularly Ron because he'd served the church so faithfully, and we were determined not to give up. Ron went to see his vicar in West Boldon, who told him there was no reason for the Rev Henderson to refuse to christen Colin, and that he would personally write to the Bishop of Jarrow to make sure it happened. He was as good as his word and within a day or two the Bishop had sent a message to Rev Henderson telling him he had to carry out the ceremony.

He complied with the order, though clearly he wasn't happy. One afternoon, before the christening, he arrived at my grandmother's door and rattled the 'sneck' (the latch) before letting himself in without being asked. He was that kind of person. Once inside he began to go through the list of proposed godparents. He approved of my friend Muriel because she, like me, had been in the church choir. He was less happy about one of Ron's choices, Bill Bruce, who was a fellow GCHQ employee but wouldn't be able to make the christening on the day. Pursing his lips, Rev Henderson asked me if this man was a regular communicant.

"Oh yes," I replied, "he certainly is. I can vouch for that."

Rev Henderson grudgingly agreed to allow Bill to be godparent by proxy. Little did he know that while Bill was indeed a regular church-goer, it was in the Roman Catholic tradition!

Back in Scotland we realised that living so far out of town would make life very difficult now we had an addition to the family. So Ron put in a claim for council accommodation and after six months we were allocated the top floor of a semi-detached house in Balgarvie Crescent. It wasn't ideal – the childless couple who lived downstairs warned us that our baby shouldn't make any noise – but it did have hot and cold water, a gas oven, a gas boiler for boiling clothes and a coal fire with a back boiler to provide hot water.

By and large we were happy there, and even the downstairs couple came to love our little boy. After two years there Ron was posted to Beverley, in East Yorkshire, and yet again we were on the move, though that didn't bother me much. I liked change and I didn't mind moving from Scotland to be back in England. That said, Ron had found us a place that really wasn't to my liking – the landlady was unpleasant and full of rules and regulations – so we gave notice to quit almost immediately and found a lovely ground floor flat in a big Victorian semi. As ever, we were short of money but that didn't seem to matter and when Colin was four we decided he might like a little brother or sister. In time, our next son, Gordon, was born and he was a very big and contented baby - as long as he was fed on time!

It was around this period that Ron began to suffer very badly with a stomach ulcer caused by the demands of shift work. His life was made miserable with pain and he could barely concentrate on his work. He was forever having time off, so his doctor recommended that he have an operation to remove the ulcerated part of the stomach. Neither of us realised just what a serious operation this was and he was very ill after the surgery, his stomach filling with blood after one of the veins had not been properly fastened off. He had a lot of blood transfusions and lost so much weight that he was just seven stones when he left hospital. He was off work for a whole year but made good progress once he was at home again. He never again put on a lot of weight but he was lucky to be alive and, finally, had been cured of his ulcers.

I will conclude this chapter how I started it: with some more words from Ron about the secretive and sometimes downright strange work he was engaged in:

We settled into Beverley really well and I enjoyed my job, which was quite a departure from what I had been doing in Brora and Cupar. Almost overnight I had become a D/F expert. 'D/F' is an abbreviation for Direction Finding and I had become a radio direction finder operator. Beverley was one of a network of D/F stations across the UK and our network was Thurso, Beverley, Ivychurch in Kent and St Erth in Cornwall.

We were charged with keeping track of the Russian Army. The intercept stations would pick up signals and wanted to make sure they were still in the same location. That's where we came in. First, the intercepted signals would be fed by landline to GCHQ Cheltenham and fed out to the D/F network. We were given the frequency of the transmission and had to tune to it and match up our radio receiver signal with the one on the landline, then take a bearing on it. These bearings would be passed on to V52 Cheltenham, along with the bearings from the rest of the network, and plotted on a large-scale map to get a 'cocked hat' fix.

Of course, this is a very laborious old-fashioned way compared with modern GPS that are much easier to operate than our miles-from-anywhere RDF stations, which were huts filled with radio equipment sat on top of a big wire mesh called an earth net, plus four pole aerials in a compound. You manned the station yourself, so you couldn't be of a nervous disposition.

One night, I was there alone and the person I'd taken the shift over from had left the compound gate open. There were often spells of inactivity when one could cat-nap and on this occasion I was just dropping off when this terrible twanging, like the devil's own guitar, brought me to my senses. I have never been so scared in my life. It was very dark, with no lights outside, and I couldn't see a thing.

Eventually I plucked up courage to switch my lights out, even as this awful noise grew louder. It was at the time of the first Russian space flight and I thought they'd put a space monster down to get me! By this time I thought I needed help so I reported what was happening to my controller at HQ and they alerted the local police. True to form they took an hour to get there and as they roared across the field, sirens blaring, I saw in the headlights that a cow was trapped in my earth net. I had to put up with an awful lot of ragging after that, and 'Robbie's spaceman' was the talk of GCHQ for a long time.

Chapter 10 – New Horizons

It wasn't easy looking after a poorly husband, a new baby and a small boy but back in those days you just got on with it and somehow managed. Ron blamed shift work for his ulcer but I wonder whether the cause of it stretched all the way back to his work in the shipyard before he was called up.

Whatever the reason, he suffered no more stomach pain following the operation. At some stage during his recuperation I'd gone up to Durham again with the boys to visit Auntie Eadie, cousin Norrie and my sister/cousin Edith. As ever, we had a good time and when I left, I remember thinking that hopefully, some day in the future, I would be able to tell Edith that she was in fact my sister and that she might enjoy a good relationship with the two nephews she didn't know she had.

By this time Edith was a schoolteacher (as was Norrie) and was a real arty type. She loved theatre, music and ballet, and was a big fan of Margot Fonteyn, to whom she wrote letters. She used to travel down to London on occasions to attend first nights and she was becoming an adventurous and cultured young woman.

One morning, in the first week of December 1955, we received a knock at our door in Beverley. Ron answered it to find a policeman on the step. He asked if I was in and when Ron said I wasn't (I'd probably gone out shopping with Colin and Gordon) the police officer told him that there had been a crash, and that my sister Edith and cousin Norrie had both been killed. When I arrived home it was down to Ron to tell me the dreadful news.

Initially I was so shocked that I thought they might have been caught up in a recent train crash in Barnes, near London, in which 13 people had died. You have to remember that news travelled far less quickly then and because Edith had recently been to London to the opening of a new theatre I assumed she had been caught up in this terrible event.

Finally we got word from Durham that she, Norrie and a friend had all been killed in a car crash in the city. It was December 5, a very icy morning, and the three had been waiting for a bus to take them to their respective workplaces. Because it was cold the buses were full and several went past without stopping. Norrie had passed her test and owned an Austin A40, so she suggested that three of them drive into work instead.

Norrie and the friend worked at the same school so the idea was to drop off Edith first. They were coming down Gilesgate Bank, a steep hill, when they encountered a bus full of miners coming from the opposite direction. Perhaps the road was narrow, or perhaps Norrie wasn't such an experienced driver. Anyway, it seemed that she braked suddenly, skidded on a patch of ice and the car went straight into the side of the bus. Edith's neck was broken and she died immediately. Norrie and the other girl were taken to hospital but all attempts to save them failed and they both died later that day. Edith was 21, Norrie 24 and the other girl about 20. It was the most awful tragedy to hit our family and particularly poignant for me because I would now never be able to tell Edith that she was my sister.

Of course, I was expected to attend the funeral so I left the children with Ron and made my way to Durham. When I arrived, Aunt Eadie was in a terrible state, fainting everywhere, and Uncle Billy was so upset that he was talking about throwing himself off a bridge into the river. Even so, Aunt Eadie still had time to demonstrate her snobbish side. I'd arrived with my hair in rollers and a sort of turban around it – quite a fashionable look then. As soon as she saw me, Eadie said, "What on earth's the matter with you, Olive? Have you got a bad head or something?" I took no notice, simply putting her rudeness down to grief.

The funeral was terribly sad, of course, because the girls were so young. Afterwards, Aunt Eadie came up to me, threw her arms around me in a dramatic gesture and said, "Well, it's just you and me now, Olive, so we must stick together."

"Oh no," I replied. "I'm afraid it's too late for that."

She looked like she'd been slapped in the face and she turned away, looking for someone else to comfort her. Perhaps I was harsh, but she had completely denied me the opportunity to get to know Edith as a sister, through no fault of my own. She never asked after me, Ron or the children and I'd had enough of her snobbish ways. I understood that she and Uncle Billy had been through a terrible ordeal and I felt for them that way, but I couldn't be some kind of substitute daughter.

After the funeral I came home to East Boldon and stayed with gran, now well into her 80s, for a few days. Christmas was approaching and she knew that I had to go back to Ron and the children, but she seemed loathe to say goodbye. As I crossed the road for the bus stop I turned around and saw her pulling back the curtains to get a better look. She waved and I waved, then the curtains were drawn again and in a few minutes the bus came to take me to the train station, and home to Beverley. I journeyed back somewhat heavy of heart and, in a way, it wasn't a huge surprise when, in the early hours of Christmas morning, I received a telegram to say that gran had died the day before and her funeral would be on Boxing Day.

Even now Christmas Day can be very quiet but in 1955 there was nothing happening, outside of a church visit and Christmas lunch. We had no car, there were no local buses to a rail connection and there were no banks open in which to withdraw money. You had to be resourceful, so after the children had opened their presents I went round to the lady next door, explained my circumstances, and asked if I could borrow some money from her. Somehow I got to Beverley station (I probably walked!) and caught the train to Newcastle from there, having spent two hours waiting for a connection at York. At Newcastle I caught the train to East Boldon and from there I walked to my cousin Elsie's. I was shattered by the time I arrived, but I stayed with her until after the funeral and once again made a heavy-hearted journey back to Ron and the children.

I just want to go back in time to say something more about my situation with my sister, Edith. Ron had always known about it, and how I was never to refer to her as 'sister'. As the years went by I began to think more about this strange situation and of course I was fully aware that there was another sister floating about somewhere. This was June, Edith's twin, and ever since she'd been spirited away from the nursing home there'd been no mention of her whatsoever. I didn't know whether she was alive or dead – though I presumed it was the former. I mentioned this to Ron one day and he suggested that I write a letter to the local paper in Newcastle to see if anyone might have any idea as to her whereabouts.

It was a good idea and I thought carefully about it before deciding not to bother. My grandma was still alive, as was Edith, and I didn't want to upset anyone. Even after their deaths I thought twice about it because there were still living relatives who wouldn't want this publicised. So I thought no more about it until much later in my life, and I'll tell you about it when the time comes!

Meanwhile we had our own busy lives to get on with – and once again we were on the move. By this time Ron had fully recovered and was back at work, to be told that he was to be posted to Ivychurch, in Kent. We were sad to say goodbye to Beverley – we had a nice house there and lots of lovely friends – but I was always up for a move to somewhere different. Ron used to say that I had gypsy blood in me. Well, I don't know if that's true or not but I certainly looked forward to settling somewhere new, and Kent was no exception. We were offered a council house and we hoped it would be as nice as the one we were leaving. Unfortunately it wasn't, but it would do us for the time being.

By this time we'd acquired our first car. Perhaps the experience of trying to get to East Boldon from Beverley on Christmas Day had sealed the decision. In any case we purchased an ex-Post Office van that Ron painted a different colour and we visited local scrapyards to get various replacement parts that were missing from it. It was a bit of a wreck but it was so handy for ferrying the children around and carrying the shopping.

Mind you, we weren't used to long journeys and so the trip down to Kent from Beverley was trying, to say the least. There were no motorways then, of course, so it was a very long trip indeed, particularly when myself, Ron, Ron's mother (who had offered to help us move) and the two boys were squashed in around our possessions. At this point Ron had never driven in the dark and when he put the car's headlights on he found they were as good as useless. We had to drive through the Blackwall Tunnel in this state and it's a miracle we didn't crash. As it was, Gordon was sick during the journey into Kent and it seemed that the car's brakes weren't as good as they should be. After seven hours or so of this Ron really had had enough and so we pulled in at Ashford for a night in a cheap boarding house, completing our journey the following day.

Over time we settled into our new place in the village of Appledore (not to be confused with the town of the same name in Devon). We found another school for Colin, and Gordon joined him shortly afterwards. In the summer of 1960 I was pregnant again, and on January 31, 1961, I gave birth to another boy, whom we called Nigel. This was the third and final addition to our family.

While life at home was good, Ron's work was throwing up a few challenges. The boss at Ivychurch was an odd fella and from the minute Ron arrived, he seemed to have it in for him. The station itself was in a remote part of Romney Marsh and this man ran it like it was his own personal kingdom. When they weren't spying on the Russians the staff kept a coop of chickens, feeding and tending to them until they went to market, with everyone sharing in the proceeds. Ron thought this was most strange and had absolutely no interest in minding chickens when he should be working. He told the boss this and immediately an atmosphere sprang up between them.

Ron was concerned that everyone else at the station seemed to go along with whatever the boss said, and he began to feel like the odd one out. I remember speaking to a few of the wives about the situation but they just laughed, and I had the sensation that no one was willing to rock the boat. It appeared that the boss was moonlighting by cleaning windows and employing a gang of window-cleaners, but even that wasn't seen to be anything out of the ordinary.

Ron would come home after his shifts regaling me with stories of his boss's eccentricity; for example, instead of pinning messages to the staff notice board he would stick them behind the toilet door 'so more people will take notice of them.' Ron thought all this carry-on was ridiculous but the man obviously felt threatened and soon he began to pick on Ron. This became so bad that an adverse report the boss had written about Ron was picked up by very senior GCHQ staff and Ron was summoned to a meeting at a nearby air force base that he'd previously never visited.

Well, I wanted to support Ron in what we both saw as an injustice that was being perpetrated against him, so on the day of the meeting we all went to the airbase in the van. When we arrived they wouldn't let me or the children any further than the front gate, so I had to deal with two small boys and a baby while Ron went in to explain himself.

When he finally emerged he was red in the face and fuming. It seemed his version of events hadn't been believed and he'd had some kind of disciplinary hearing. 'They wouldn't even let me have a union rep in there,' he said as he climbed into the driver's seat. That would've really upset Ron, because he was a real one for the union he'd helped to found. He was huffing and puffing all the way home and I hardly dared ask him for any more details.

It was disappointing for all of us because we were hoping that we'd be posted abroad. Being in the Navy, Ron had long been bitten by the travel bug and I was keen to experience at least some of the places that Ron had talked about with such vivid memories. Now it looked like this was in jeopardy, because the upshot of the hearing was that Ron would now have to be subjected to close assessment at a facility near St Albans. He would be taken off the overseas postings list until his reports had improved.

I was very upset by this. I thought he'd lose his job and I wondered where we would live then. We had no house of our own – every place we'd ever lived in had been rented, either privately or through the council. Ron, however, didn't seem to think the situation was quite as bad as was painted. Still, we had to pack up everything and move to Hertfordshire while we awaited the outcome of Ron's trial period.

Ron's instincts were right. He went to St Albans for a few days alone, and when he came back he was full of smiles. The man in charge there was an old mate from the Navy – and it turned out that this man had about as much respect and liking for Ron's old boss in Kent as he did!

"He's told me he can't stand him either," he said, "and that I've not got to worry about a thing." And the next we knew, Ron was being posted to Singapore, and a whole new life would be waiting for us in just a short few months' time.

So on that basis we moved to a place in Bletchley, close to Woburn Abbey, the Duke of Bedford's estate, while Ron went on a course that would train him for life and work in the Far East. The house was big, and overlooked the estate. There was a lovely kitchen and two excellent bedrooms but apart from a coal fire there was no heating and we were right in the middle of a very cold winter. Gordon was a bed wetter and so the lack of drying facilities made life very difficult. Everything froze in the house and I seemed to be spending forever just keeping the fire going.

By now, Colin was about 10 and coming close to finishing primary school. He and Gordon went to a school nearby, and Gordon would stay in Colin's class at the end of the day while they waited for me to pick them up. Gordon was bright and chirpy and when Colin's class was asked a question by their teacher, he would stick up his hand and answer ahead of everyone else – much to the embarrassment of his older brother.

As I mentioned, we had a good view of the Woburn estate from our kitchen and one day I spotted a deer close to the kitchen window. It was a bright, cold day and the animal could be seen very clearly so I lifted up Gordon and Nigel to see for themselves. "Look, here's little Bambi," I said. Next second there was a terrific bang and the poor creature dropped down dead, shot by a gamekeeper I expect. The kids went into hysterics and I'm not surprised. It really was quite a shocking thing to see.

A few weeks before we were due to embark for Singapore we

all had to have some terrible injections for diseases including bubonic plague and yellow fever. I was very worried about how the children would react to these injections, as they were known to knock even the strongest of military men off their feet. We decided to have them in stages – I would have mine along with the children while Ron would have his after just in case we were both knocked out. Gordon and Colin had theirs first followed by Nigel, who had a special injection formulated for his young age. He was fine but Gordon and Colin were quite poorly. Colin fell asleep in the doctor's chair and continued sleeping for about 24 hours. When he awoke he was fine except for a very swollen arm. Gordon ran a high temperature, was sick and complained of headaches. His arm was also swollen. I was not too bad at all and managed, like Colin, to sleep it off. Ron was also alright, apart from a swollen arm. We took this as a good sign and finally we were summoned to Tilbury Dock in London, where, in a few days' time, we would be stepping aboard the SS Himalaya for the long voyage to Singapore, via Gibraltar, the Suez Canal and Bombay, and a whole new way of life.

Chapter 11 – The voyage out

There was a two or three-day gap between us leaving St Albans and boarding the ship, so we were scheduled to move into a hotel in London for this short duration. By this time we'd sold the old Post Office van and had bought a Morris Oxford, which was to be stowed aboard the ship so that we could use it in Singapore.

On the day we left St Albans I went to get my hair done at a local hairdresser's. Ron had the kids in the car and he'd just parked up outside the finance company to make the last remaining payment on the vehicle. After he'd done this he was due to pick me up and we'd be on our way. Ron left the children in the car but when he came out of the office a terrible sight awaited him. It was a bitterly cold day and a coal lorry had skidded on some ice and smashed right into the side of the Oxford. Its flank was almost ripped off, the windows were smashed and the door wouldn't open properly. How the children survived is something of a miracle, because there were no seatbelts fitted in those days. But they did survive, and were uninjured, and given what happened to my sister and cousin in Durham, that has always been something to be very thankful for.

Of course, Ron now had a problem because the car was due to be loaded on the ship at Tilbury. The police were keen to take the vehicle away for examination but Ron refused, explaining we were now on our way to Singapore. So in double-quick time he found someone who could bodge the car up by sealing the broken side with either plastic or polystyrene – I forget which. Meanwhile, I was outside the hairdresser's in the freezing cold, wondering where everybody was. When Ron finally caught up with me and told me the sorry tale I was in shock, and panicking that somehow we might literally 'miss the boat' because of what had happened.

We drove down to London very carefully. By this time it was dark and we were beginning to relax a little when a red car suddenly came down one of the exit roads off the M1 the wrong way and nearly hit us. What a day that was! By the end of it we felt lucky to be alive.

The poor battered car was dropped off at its embarkation point and we took a taxi to our hotel on the Cromwell Road. When we tried to book in, the manager told us that this place was reserved for higher-ranking civil servants only. Well, after the day we'd had we stood our ground and the manager relented, being ex-civil servant himself. We were glad to get into bed, and by now you'd hope our troubles were over… until Gordon started complaining of having a sore throat and swollen glands. The following day a doctor came from Harley Street (at huge expense) and diagnosed a case of the mumps. That was handy!

Mumps or no mumps, we had to be on that boat and so I decided not to tell anyone about his condition. Strangely enough, the whole family's excitement at seeing the SS Himalaya berthed at Tilbury, waiting for us to board her, seemed to alleviate Gordon's condition and by the time we were on board his glands were almost back to normal.

As ever, Ron had to attend a briefing so the rest of us were left to explore the ship. There was a playroom for children, complete with a resident nanny, so I left the three children with her while I continued my wanders. Little did I know that unwittingly I'd deposited them in first class! I also needed the loo and when I came out I mentioned to Ron that there seemed to be basins on the walls. He eyed me suspiciously, and more so when I innocently wondered if they were footbaths. "Olive, I think you've been in the men's," he said. I was rather more careful after that.

All our furniture and possessions we didn't need on the voyage had been stowed on another ship. Everything else was in an enormous trunk, which seemed to be full of toys that the kids had got for Christmas. Ron and I had a cabin and the boys shared an adjacent one.

The ship weighed anchor and to the sounds of cheering from the dockside we set off on our adventure. Quickly we had to get used to the system of bells employed to muster everyone for their meals. We would be woken to a knock on the door and a steward standing there with fruit and tea on a trolley. Then it was the first ding-dong-ding! and the children would be sent off for breakfast in the playroom. Next it was our turn, followed by another ding-dong-ding! at 11am, signifying that the children's lunch was ready. Then it was our lunch, and another clanging of bells at 3.30pm to tell us it was teatime. This was followed by the children's evening meal and finally, at 7pm, it was our dinner, which was always formal.

Naturally, we'd not been used to this at all. Ron had to wear a dinner suit (in fact, it was his black wedding suit, so it came in useful after all…) and I had but one dress. As ever, we'd just have to manage until we came to the first port of call, Gibraltar. Having children, our dining arrangements weren't as relaxed as other people's. The boys were full of energy and although a steward was meant to be looking after them in our cabin during our dinner, we were often called away from the table to settle them down. We'd do that – only to be called out again ten minutes later to repeat the same thing.

The journey was quite rough at some points and there was plenty of seasickness as people adjusted to life onboard a boat. Far from being scared by high seas, the boys thought it was the best fun. As the boat plunged downwards into a wave, they'd run against the direction of the ship, then the other way as the ship came back up again.

We arrived in Gibraltar after a few days and were relieved to be able to leave the boat for a few hours, as the boys were going stir crazy by this time. We discovered cheap watches for sale and Ron bought one for each of us. We thought we'd won the pools as wristwatches were very expensive in the UK then. There was also time for evening dress shopping and because the Foreign Office insisted ladies buy only pure silk (oh, the rules and regulations back then…) I was only able to run to a couple.

After Gibraltar we headed for the Red Sea and the Suez Canal. One night, as we were leaving the Med, I woke up and noticed that everything seemed to be so still and quiet. I mentioned this to Ron, who suggested that we go up on deck. So we did, and the moonlit sea, so calm and dark, was absolutely beautiful. 'This is the start of the good life,' I thought. And I was right.

Quite a few people got off to see the Pyramids when we had a brief stop-over in Port Said, Egypt, but our family budget couldn't run to this. Nevertheless, we were entertained by an Arab nicknamed 'the gully-gully man' who got on many of the passenger ships travelling up and down the canal. He was dressed in all the fancy robes and he carried with him a company of chicks, which he brought out from everywhere. The children were fascinated by him, and using sleight of hand he'd draw birds from behind their ears.

When we arrived in Colombo Ron's pay was waiting for him,

so finally we weren't having to watch every penny. The next stop was to be Bombay. Before the voyage I'd been in touch with my cousin Kathleen, who'd married an Indian man called Ajoy and was now living in Bombay. She'd been in the RAF and had met her husband-to-be while they were both at Newcastle University. They'd become friendly, then romantically entangled and finally married in Bombay. Kathleen worked at the British Embassy and led quite a luxurious life. As we sailed along the west coast of India I became excited at the prospect of seeing Kathleen and setting foot in India for the first time.

I got up very early on the morning the ship docked and went on deck. It was 3am, warm and quiet, and you could literally smell India – a smell of many people intermingled with sweet flowers and exotic spices. I saw men sleeping by the many bollards that lined the side of the dock, just resting before the day's work started. I could hardly believe that I was here, a girl from East Boldon who'd lost her parents so young.

For some reason we weren't able to leave the ship straight away and we were becoming frustrated at the delay. By this time the dock was full of people rushing about. I scanned the mass of bodies along the dock, trying to identify Kathleen, but it was impossible from the height we were at. So we clambered down the gangways until we were just one deck up and then it was easy to see Kathleen and her children. They were waving and shouting but we couldn't make out what they were saying. Just then, an Indian man came up to me and asked if I was Mrs Roberts. It was Ajoy, of course, and by some miracle he'd managed to locate us. He was working as a surveyor on the docks and he told us to follow him, which we did, and we were off the ship long before anyone else.

It was a joy to be reunited with Kathleen and she was so pleased to be able to show us around her adopted city. Ajoy had a car and driver waiting but we were very happy to just walk and experience on foot everything Bombay had to offer. I needed some shorts for the children as we were now well into the tropics, so Ajoy simply dived into the nearest tailor's and the trio were measured for shorts which would be made 'in the day – no problem'. And they were!

We visited the Taj Mahal Hotel, which had some strange rules about which days they served certain kinds of food. We were a bit puzzled by this and besides, the kids only wanted egg and chips. So that's what was ordered and when it came it appeared that we'd all got a portion. Such a funny thing to happen in a genuinely posh hotel. After this we strolled through a beautiful garden and into a park which had a signpost that read 'Parents only allowed if children want them to come in'. The kids thought that was great. Following a visit to the beach we drove back to Kathleen and Ajoy's behind a horse and cart that couldn't have been going more than a couple of miles an hour.

Before we arrived at their house, Kathleen wanted to take us to a local cake shop, so Ajoy stopped there, and as Kathleen, Ron and I walked down the step into the shop, a carpet of flies greeted me. Kathleen ordered, and as the shop staff placed the cakes into bags, they were blowing the flies off them. I was horrified, I must admit, but Kathleen didn't bat an eyelid. When we got home I warned my boys not to eat them, and that I would have the cakes so as not to upset her.

Meanwhile Ajoy was wondering if Ron and I had our passports with us. We did, and Ajoy seemed delighted that we would be able to buy some whisky, which wasn't sold to local people and was kept at the nearby police station. So Ajoy and I went off in the car to the station. There, a store was unlocked like a prison door and following Ajoy's whispered instructions I ordered whisky and brandy which he later paid for, of course. Ajoy also suggested Ron getting the Morris Oxford off the ship because he thought it may fetch a good price in the city. Ron seemed interested but I didn't like the sound of it.

Anyway, Kathleen was offering to make us all egg and chips (again) but Ajoy would have none of it. He wanted us to try Indian food for the first time and he went out and came back with red Tandoori Chicken. Well, it was like nothing I'd ever tasted and I can't say my first experience was a pleasant one. It was red hot and the kids were pulling some very strange faces as they tasted it. So it was back to the drawing board, and Kathleen's egg and chips. How English we all were then…

To entertain Kathleen and Ajoy's children we'd brought some of our boys' toy cars from the boat. However, they were battery-operated and the kids could only play with them for a limited amount of time because replacement batteries were almost impossible to find in India at that time. Also, I think Nigel was keen to have his cars back intact.

We were quite late getting back to the ship, not helped by an Indian man whom Ron had befriended on the way out. He'd disembarked at Bombay and was now waiting by the gangplank to say goodbye. The crew stood around agitatedly as this man said his elaborate farewells, and as soon as we were clear, the gangplank was pulled up and off we went, headed for Penang.

We had made friends with a couple on the ship who were going to Malaya to work. They had three children, including an 18-year-old girl called Sally. They were leaving the ship at Penang so we agreed to join them at the Eastern and Oriental Hotel, where they would be staying temporarily, and have a meal with them before saying goodbye. As the ship arrived in Penang I went up on the top deck again and I don't think I've ever seen a more beautiful sight. It was early morning; the sea was as calm as a millpond and the city's buildings were reflected in it. There was a smell wafting across from the land of warm spices and frangipani flowers, and the most glorious empty beaches you've ever seen. I have been to lots of places since Penang, and have been back there since, but never captured that feeling again. It was as if I was experiencing what the clipper ships must have seen as they called in to pick up spices for the East India Company.

We went ashore and were very impressed by the size of the Eastern and Oriental, one of the world's greatest. The kids were amazed and delighted by the huge old cannons that were placed outside the hotel. We were equally impressed by the huge lounge and its ceiling full of fans. The room was so big that the chairs and tables looked miniscule. After a lovely meal we said goodbye to our friends, promising to return when we'd settled into our new environment. Then we returned to the ship, which would sail down the Strait of Malacca to Singapore, our final destination.

CHAPTER 12 – SETTLING INTO SINGAPORE

As might be expected, the end of a long voyage was a whirl of packing, form-filling, marshalling children and general chaos. The trunks were collected and the official documents handed to certain dignitaries who'd arrived on the Himalaya the previous day. Passports, customs forms and immigration documents were all needed; it was as if we'd been invaded overnight by a secret army.

Alongside the officials came all sorts of weird and wonderful people wearing sarongs and saris, turbans and topis. Some had baskets on their heads and others carried clothes, food, cases, trunks and everything else you can imagine. We were a bit worried by all the strangers and noise, so when there was a knock on our cabin door it was with great care that we opened it.

Imagine our surprise and relief, then, to see Ron's cousin, Johnnie Hamill, and his wife Esther standing there with open arms to welcome us to the Far East. Johnnie was in the RAF and it was the first time I'd ever seen air force tropical dress, so at first I just didn't recognise them. Once I did, I was delighted to see them.

Ron was called to a briefing in the First-Class lounge so Esther, Johnnie, the children and I went to get some drinks. However, we'd been used to paying in sterling throughout the voyage but now we were at our destination it had all changed. Luckily, Uncle Johnnie was carrying Singapore Dollars and he was pleased to buy the kids Coca-Cola all round. During the briefing Ron was given an amount of Singapore Dollars, so soon we were poring over this strange money that we'd be using over the next three years.

Getting off the ship was not an easy process and I had to say goodbye to Johnnie and Esther. He needed to get back to RAF Tengah, where he was based, and besides, a lot of GCHQ people had come down to meet the boat, telling us that we would be transported to our hotel in a fleet of cars. Somehow it was decided that the women and children would travel separately from the men, and to my dismay Ron and I were split up.

The children and I were herded into the back of a car by an Irish couple. When we set off they started to tell us about Singapore – and they were the most miserable, depressing people I'd ever met. "Oh, it's an awful place," the woman replied when I asked them what living in Singapore was like. "It's terrible," the man added in a droning voice, "mark my words, you'll wish you'd never bothered."

Well, what a start! And to cap it all, as I was sitting in the back feeling worse by the minute, who should sail past in an open-topped sports car but Ron. There he was, in the passenger seat, his feet up and smoking a cigarette like he was having the time of his life. Eventually I tuned out of my hosts' dreary conversation and concentrated on the sights and sounds of the new country flashing before my eyes. It fascinated me, and immediately I felt much better.

Finally we arrived at the New Earth Hotel, which Colin and Gordon immediately re-named 'The Death Hotel' as their spelling was a bit wonky. We would be staying here while we looked for a suitable place to live. We were glad of a place to rest our heads but this hotel wasn't the best place for us. It was stuffed full of Army and RAF officers and their wives, all of whom seemed rather unfriendly to say the least. They were protective of their customs and ways, and we couldn't seem to step over the invisible line which separated Them from Us. They were completely indifferent to us and it was at that point I realised that I was a Civilian, and therefore very different from military types. I thought I was just plain old me, and assumed the rest of the world felt the same.

The climate and environment also took some getting used to. I would never put my foot down at the bottom of the bed in case a snake was lurking there and I was terrified that the children would get food poisoning. The air was hot and muggy, but every time I went into the room the windows were shut firmly. I couldn't understand this so I'd open them again immediately. I'd leave the room and come back later to find that once again, they'd been shut tight. I became fed up of this so I asked a hotel employee the reason for the windows being closed. He had to explain about air conditioning, and how it didn't work when the windows were wide open. Air conditioning... well, that was a new one on me!

We spent a couple of months in the hotel before being told by Johnnie that he'd found a bungalow in Serangoon, and it was ours if we wanted it. We looked at it and it seemed perfect for our needs. Ron didn't want to live in a barracks surrounded by people he worked with every day. He was after a more authentic experience of the country and he insisted that we live where the locals did. This would set a pattern that we'd stick to right through our travels with Ron's job.

We were very happy to leave the hotel behind – it was stuffy in all senses of the word – and by this time our poor battered Morris Oxford had been taken off the ship and was waiting in a garage for us to pick it up. I liked the bungalow but wasn't over-keen on the flying ants that seemed to invade it regularly. For a few nights, particularly when Ron was at work, I was also extremely disturbed by what I thought were the noises of elephants and big cats, particularly tigers, in close proximity to the house. This really troubled me and I wondered if I was hearing things. Finally, I mentioned it to Johnnie. "Don't worry, Olive," he said, laughing, "you aren't going mad. There are elephants and tigers around here... because there's a bloody circus just up the road!" Oh, the English abroad!

We hired an 'amah' (the Singaporean equivalent of an au pair), a Malay girl called Emmie. She was young and pretty and she soon settled in, taking it upon herself to look after Nigel. She genuinely loved him, and in a way she really helped us to settle in and get used to this strange new environment. Emmie was particularly helpful when it came to school arrangements for Colin and Gordon. Ron and his work colleagues sorted out school places for them in Changi and all Emmie and I had to do was get them to the school bus on time.

As we know, getting schoolboys out of bed and into uniforms is no easy task, but Emmie seemed to have persuasive skills. On their first day we accompanied them on the school bus (called a gharrie) to Seletar Camp, because they were attending an army school. I was amazed to see their classrooms had no windows as such, just openings in the walls, and what looked like straw roofs. I felt very lonely and guilty as I watched Colin and Gordon get their names pinned on their new school uniforms (white short-sleeved shirts and khaki shorts) which had been starched stiffly by Emmie, before being marched off to their new classrooms. I burst into tears and had to be comforted by the Headmistress. She was used to this kind of behaviour, telling me it was only natural when you considered we were so unused to this kind of environment.

I wasn't the only one. Other newly arrived British women living nearby seemed as confused as I was. I remember packing the boys off on the bus one morning, and I was still in my nightie. There was a knock at the door and an English neighbour was standing there, also in her nightie. "What time is it?" she asked. "I think it's about 8am," I said. "Oh," she replied, "I'm so sorry for calling round early. I just can't judge what time it is out here." "Come in," I said, "and let's have breakfast." And we were confused together!

Our battered Morris Oxford car was picked up from the ship by a local man who did the garden around our bungalow. He spoke good English and followed Ron's instructions about collecting the car to the letter, but when he came back he was sweating buckets. Finally, we worked out that the car had gone on to the ship at Tilbury with the heating on (because it was winter, of course) and the heating switch hadn't been turned off before the ignition. So it had come on automatically, and because heating wasn't needed in Singapore this poor man had no way of knowing why the car was so hot inside.

Eventually Ron got the Morris fixed and he decided to apply for a new car, but his application was turned down on the grounds he'd agreed to bring his own car out. Ron was persistent, however, and finally they relented and let us buy a new car – a Triumph Herald.

After a while we decided to move out of the bungalow because Ron had spotted a bigger house advertised in the property section of the Singapore Straits Times. It belonged to a Chinese millionaire who'd been the victim of a ransom kidnapping, which appeared to be quite common at that time. The house was in Siglap, by the coast, and was probably more than we could afford in rent, but as Ron said, "While we're here, let's enjoy it." And he was right. Lots of people put up with living in semi-hovels just to save up money they could bring home at the end of their tour, but we were there as much for the experience as anything else. And Siglap Avenue, where the house was located, was like millionaire's row. It was built in an Art Deco style (though it wasn't of that period – in fact, it was quite a new place) and it was huge. The boys adored it, and I remember Nigel's face as he tore round the garden on a go-kart. He loved this vehicle, and was even more delighted when, one Christmas, he received a brand-new one. Except that it wasn't brand new – Ron had taken it apart and repainted it.

So we took the house on, and at the same time I joined the Singapore Swimming Club. This was an old-fashioned British Empire institution, grand and beautiful, and an absolute pleasure to visit. As well as swimming they had lots of activities (for example outdoor film shows) and it was the place to be. Nothing as vulgar as money was ever flashed around – if you wanted drinks or food you just signed a chit and paid at the end of the month. And yes, I adjusted to this new and quite posh way of life very easily! Life was good – I'd no need to work, and I had someone to help me with the cooking, cleaning and minding the children.

On a typical day, if Ron was at home and the kids were at school, we'd go to the Swimming Club, then to the beach or out shopping. Robinson's was the big fashionable store then, the equivalent of Harrod's I suppose. We'd pay a visit there then look at all the old streets and smaller local shops. We didn't have to be back for the kids coming home because Emmie was there, looking after Nigel while waiting for the school bus to arrive with Colin and Gordon on board. If Ron was at work I'd go down to the Swimming Club or meet with other GCHQ wives for coffee mornings or shopping trips. It was a good life, well-paid and far different from the somewhat bleak day-to-day existence many of us knew back in Britain at that time. I appreciated every minute of my good fortune.

The house was full of Chinese-style fixtures, fittings and

furniture, including an enormous fish tank which spanned the length of one room, dividing it in two. It was full of tropical fish and the boys were fascinated by it, especially Colin. By this time he'd got heavily into fishing and we'd often take him, Gordon and Nigel, to a local fish farm where you were almost guaranteed to catch something. One day Colin caught a fish and insisted on bringing it back home for the tank. So we found a jam jar to transport the fish, and then placed it into the tank, where it grew... and grew... and grew. At first we couldn't work out why it was growing so quickly until one day we saw Colin's fish with one of the larger of the Angel Fish in its mouth. By now, we'd come to accept that we had a hungry catfish in our tank and we resigned ourselves to replacing all its victims before we left Singapore. We did replace them but at some stage we decided to clean the tank out. To do this, you had to pull out a plug on the side of the tank and allow the water to drain away. It was an ingenious system but unfortunately we forgot to take the fish out first. By the time Colin and Gordon had got their fishing nets to the gushing water we'd again lost a fair few beautiful fish.

Every week, a night market would set up along Siglap Avenue. These are a common feature right across the Far East and they sold absolutely everything. The stalls were illuminated by kerosene lamps and it was all chaos and noise. Woe betides if you needed to get your car out of your drive – the market stretched right along the road and lasted all evening. A record stall at the night market was the first place I ever heard the Beatles. They'd only just become famous but already their music had made it to Singapore.

Our next-door neighbours were local people. The husband had an unpronounceable name so we called him Mr Ee for short. His wife was Malay Chinese and they had a family ranging from Nancy, a 21-year-old air stewardess for Singapore Airlines, to Jacqueline, a sweet little girl the same age as Nigel. They had a lot of servants, all of whom they referred to as 'Auntie', and they were quite traditional in that they kept up a lot of Chinese customs, like sending up prayers to the gods of the kitchen and wringing the necks of the chickens they kept before hanging them on the washing line in the heat to cure them.

They also kept dogs - small fox terrier types that were said to be good guard dogs and quite vicious. When we first moved in I remember seeing the old grandfather (who lived with them) tying them to the fence before washing them down with a hosepipe. One day, we found in our post box a letter for them that had been misdirected. Ron was posting it in their post box when one of the dogs bit him on the leg. It was only a small bite and Ron wasn't so bothered. Even so, he was concerned that the dogs might bite Nigel as he enjoyed playing with Jacqueline. So he went round and tried to make them understand, saying 'dog bite, dog bite' and showing them the wound. They didn't quite get it and it was only resolved when Nancy came around and, in perfect English, explained that her parents didn't speak English and were 'awfully sorry'.

Then it was our turn to get a dog. It seemed to be the thing to have a dog to guard the property. At the time there was an insurgency in Malaya and although we didn't see any trouble, it was all going on in the background. Ron had to be taken to work every day in a British Army truck because there was a risk he might be kidnapped. Generally we felt perfectly safe but given that the owner of our house had been kidnapped and ransomed, we didn't want to take any chances.

So we went to a local 'kampung' – a traditional village where houses are built on stilts over water – and came away with a German Shepherd puppy we named Simba. From the start we realised that while he was loving and gentle with us, he could be vicious with other people. In short, the perfect guard dog. I seem to recall that he nipped several people who came to visit, but the kids loved him and so we decided to keep him.

Mr and Mrs Ee and their family were nice neighbours. As I said, Nigel and Jacqueline got on well and when I put Nigel into school, aged four, Mrs Ee was very curious to know why we did this at such an early age. Ron explained to Mr Ee, who spoke a bit of English, that it was normal for British children to go to school at this age, and in any case it was more like a creche than a school. Mr Ee wondered if it was a Christian school, and Ron told them that yes, it was, and quite strongly Christian too because it was run by Americans.

Mr Ee was impressed enough to send Jacqueline to the same school and on the first day we took a photograph of them together, Nigel wearing a bowtie and Jacqueline in a sarong. The school must have had quite an influence on Jacqueline because one day Ron saw her swinging on the fence that separated our gardens and was concerned that she might pull it down. I was dispatched to sort it out, but when I got up to her, I couldn't say anything for laughing – the little girl was merrily swinging away while singing 'Jesus Wants Me For A Sunbeam'! I rushed inside and told Ron. "Oh god," he said, "I hope her parents don't hear her!"

On the subject of Jacqueline – and to jump ahead a little bit – some years later we visited our old house on one of our holiday tours. We stopped the car and were walking up the road when out of next door's bungalow came a girl of about 12 or 13. It was Jacqueline, and straight away she recognised us. "Auntie Olive! Uncle Ron!" she shouted, and she was so thrilled to see us. We were introduced to the occupants of our old house by a beaming Jacqueline, who couldn't stop hugging us. Then she turned to Nigel, who was accompanying us. "You're so handsome now," she said, smiling.

While we were living in Singapore there was some confrontational problem between Singapore and Indonesia, which stemmed from Indonesia's opposition to the creation of Malaysia. The net result of this were curfews, which sometimes made shopping difficult. However, this didn't seem to bother our neighbours two doors away, the Tan family, because Mr Tan was the local chief inspector of police and somehow Mrs Tan went out during the curfew without any trouble whatsoever. She'd bring back groceries for us and in return I'd make them an apple pie or some bread. Nancy told us the Tans were very impressed because they'd believed that English people only ever ate out of tins. No doubt Mrs Tan also paid plenty of 'kumshaw' for the groceries. In Chinese, kumshaw means 'grateful thanks', although we'd understand the word as being another expression for 'bribe'. Very soon, we came to realise that kumshaw needed to be paid to get anything done. And after all, Ron did want to live like the locals.

Mr Tan was a messenger for Mr Soon Guan, the millionaire who owned our house. He also owned a lot of the buses that went to and from Changi, plus the bus station too. We rarely saw him but when his daughter got married we were invited. This was a very lavish affair, including a 40-course banquet, and we were required to dress up in all our finery. Now, Ron didn't drink except for the occasional glass of whisky, but the Chinese custom at weddings was to toast the bride and groom as often as possible with the words 'Yam Sing!' They toasted with very strong rice wine and I think the powers of alcohol drew Ron and Mr Soon Guan together because they were chatting like old friends. Mr Soon Guan was keen to 'adopt' Ron into his club of rich Chinese businessmen who went all over the Far East following horse racing or gambling in the casinos. Ron wasn't quite in their financial league, nor was he a betting man, but he was flattered to be asked.

The Yam Sing-ing went on for many hours and at 3am it was time to leave the wedding. We had to drive from the city centre to where we lived in Siglap Avenue, but Ron was completely out of it and I couldn't drive. Anyway, Ron insisted and so we were weaving from side to side as we journeyed back in the early dawn. How we made it back home in one piece I don't know, but we did, and Ron slept for the whole of the following day.

On another occasion we were invited to a funeral ceremony for a relative of Mr Ee. During the ceremony we were very surprised to see a whole bus load of people arriving, each clutching a white umbrella and crying their eyes out. It was all rather odd, especially when the family themselves weren't crying at all. Later on we discovered that it was usual custom to employ people to cry at funerals on your behalf. So what we'd seen was a display from a group of professional mourners.

Then there was Chinese New Year. Presents would be sent from Mr Soon Guan and there would be more presents waiting for us at the houses of Mr Tan and Mr Ee. These usually consisted of envelopes of money for the kids, then the fireworks would start. Colin loved this; along with the local children he'd throw firecrackers into the monsoon drains and they'd go off with a huge explosion. There was also a ceremony in which wads of money were ritually burned – I never quite understood that one, but I think it was something to do with not taking money into the next world.

We had a special grocer in Singapore who also acted as a kind of banker. If you were a bit short one month he'd lend you extra and you'd pay him back when you got your groceries bill, along with the obligatory 'kumshaw'. He and his family always had a street party in Singapore for female customers, and I - along with all the other 'memsahibs' – would go along to eat course after course of Chinese food and have our fortunes told. They asked for my date of birth, and when I told them, a couple of men picked me up while I was still in my seat and carried me to the top of the table, where there was a kind of throne into which I was placed. I didn't know it at that point, but 1928 – the year of my birth – was the Year of The Dragon and I was meant to be the luckiest person there. Of course, all my friends were in hysterics at this.

I met many of these friends at the coffee mornings held in each other's houses, or at lunches at the yacht club. It must have been on one of these occasions that I heard about the delights of Bugis Street (pronounced 'Boogie Street'). "Have you been there yet, Olive?" said one of the ladies. I admitted that I hadn't, but would be interested to go there, whatever it was. Mere mention of it was accompanied by a lot of giggling, so when I got home that evening I suggested to Ron that next time we had some time off, we should visit Bugis Street.

Well, he nearly choked on his tea. "We're not going down there!" he spluttered. "Not a chance. I wouldn't dream of taking you there!"

I hardly dared ask him more about it but a bit of discreet questioning among my girlfriends revealed that it was a place full of what we'd now describe as 'ladyboys' – men who looked and dressed like women – offering dubious services to passing Naval personnel and American GIs. Needless to say, we never did go down there but I think I'd have been intrigued to see it.

Mind you, we did have some odd experiences in Singapore, including the time I was chased down the street by a mad Chinese giant. We were out shopping with some friends and were browsing the stalls when I happened to catch the eye of a huge Chinese stallholder. He was bald and full of muscles and for some reason he took an immediate dislike to me. Shouting at the top of his voice, he picked up a large chain, abandoned his stall and chased me down the street. I was so frightened that I pulled the kids into a taxi and sped away, leaving Ron and our friends to deal with this madman. My last impression of the scene was seeing Ron waving a spanner at him in an attempt to calm him down.

We never did get to the bottom of what it was that had triggered this extreme behaviour but it was terrifying at the time.

I have to say that England seemed very boring in comparison to all this, but of course most of the people we knew were British (apart from our neighbours), including Johnnie and Esther and Margaret and David Watson. Margaret was the daughter of my dear cousin Elsie, who had been so good to me when I was young. David was in the Royal Signals and was posted out to Singapore for two years. During this time cousin Elsie came to visit them and we were reunited on the other side of the world.

We also had Naval visitors if one of our warships docked at a certain time of year, particularly Christmas. I recall HMS Ark Royal coming out to visit one Christmas and we were all asked if we could billet a serviceman or two for a weekend. We accommodated two lads from the Ark Royal and they were hilarious, and great company. We took them to see the film 'Zulu', starring Michael Caine, which was just out then, and they had a nice Christmas with us.

As a 'thank you' we were invited to visit the Ark Royal just before it left port. Being a former Naval man, Ron was desperate to get on board, and as it turned out, so was Colin. So Ron contacted an officer on the ship and asked if it was alright to bring his son along. The reply was a most definite 'no', so the boys had to stay behind while we dressed up in our finery and prepared to visit the aircraft carrier.

The day we went it seemed that every dignitary in Singapore had been invited along, and I remember following behind Lee Kuan Yew, the then-Prime Minister of Singapore, and Tunku Abdul Rahman, the Prime Minister of Malaysia. Ron shook hands with the Royal Naval Admiral before we all went on to the top deck for a reception. During this, we got with a party of Naval officers and their wives, and during the conversation one of these men said, "Well, you'll never believe this, a man rang me up today

– I think he was a Scotsman – and asked if he could bring his child on board!"

Ron smiled. Situations like this never bothered him. "That was me," he said, smiling and introducing both of us. The officer looked very embarrassed, and quite rightly, but his wife went some way to defusing the situation by asking us if we were Geordies, and where were we from?

I told her I was from East Boldon and her face lit up. "Do you know the branch of Barclays Bank there?" she asked. "My father used to run that." And from there we all got along well and had a very enjoyable evening.

You'll remember that on the voyage out to Singapore we'd become friends with a family who had an 18-year-old daughter, Sally. When they departed the ship at Penang we promised to keep in touch and we did. This included several visits, and it was during one of these visits that I was told Sally had become pregnant. She'd gone out to a party with several Indian boys she knew and had fallen pregnant by one of them. Well, this was a great scandal – an unmarried white British teenage girl becoming pregnant by an Indian boy. The poor girl confided in me that she wasn't allowed out for fear she would shame her family. Ron and I felt very sorry for her and I suggested to her mother that Sally might like to visit us in Singapore.

Well, the girl's parents jumped at the chance of getting her off their hands, so she arrived and became one of the family. When it was time for her to have the baby her parents decided that she would go into a Catholic nursing home in Singapore, run by nuns. We abided by their wishes but were shocked to discover that the patients had to provide their own food, so I did a lot of cooking during her confinement. There was no question that she would be allowed to keep her baby, of course, but she was allowed to nurse the little girl for a day or two before the baby was taken away and given to adoptive parents. I went in one day to find her upset over the fact that fresh leaves had been placed over the baby's forehead. Then we found out it was a traditional Chinese remedy for overheated infants!

Eventually the baby was taken away. Sally went back to her parents in Penang and we never heard from any of them again. Presumably they just wanted to forget the whole episode. However, some years later, Ron's cousin Johnnie returned to Singapore to work after he'd retired from the RAF – he loved the place and missed it while back in England. Anyway, I believe he was guarding an RAF airfield when a young WAAF came up to him. "Hi Uncle Johnnie," she said, "it's me – Sally!" It was our friend's daughter, who by now had joined the RAF and had married. She asked how we all were and they exchanged a few pleasantries before she departed. Sadly, he never saw her again so he was unable to ask what had happened to her baby. Perhaps, though, it wouldn't have been mentioned in any circumstances.

Ron decided he'd like to sail the waters around Singapore so he bought an old clinker-built lifeboat that had definitely seen better days. It was practically derelict and he spent evenings and weekends at Changi Yacht Club, sanding it down, varnishing, painting, polishing and fitting it with masts and gunter-rigged sails. When it was ready we'd go out in it most weekends, just exploring the seas around the island and seeing where we ended up. Only Nigel, being the youngest, wore a life-jacket. No one gave much consideration to health and safety in those days, and Colin and Gordon regularly jumped off the boat and swam to the nearest island. I remember one time that Nigel suddenly decided to join them and leapt overboard without his lifejacket. Somehow he made it to the shore!

We'd often go to an island called Blakang Mati (now known as Sentosa). Then, it was a British Army base, having been used as a Japanese prisoner-of-war camp during the Second World War. The Japanese surrendered to the British there in 1945. It was off-limits to local people but we could go there because of Ron's connections with the military. We'd stop off and have a picnic before carrying on exploring.

Ron was a very enthusiastic sailor but he wasn't the best at navigating or reading the moods of the sea. I remember one time sailing around Malacca Island but missing the channel that would've taken us back to the yacht club. A huge container ship passed by and Ron was shouting at the crew members leaning over the side, asking which way Singapore was. Somehow we became terribly lost and finished up god-knows-where in Malaysia. We berthed at a yacht club so we had to leave the boat there and get a taxi back home, which took hours.

Sometimes we took out visitors. Margaret, my cousin, and her husband David came to visit and although she was very nervous about what might happen if we capsized, she agreed to a sail. Well, we didn't capsize but she screamed her head off when a British submarine unexpectedly surfaced about 200 yards from us!

We tried to see as much as possible while we were there. One of the most vivid memories is of the snake temple on Penang. The place was full of them and although the boys were excited I kept my distance from the cobras and pythons that slithered about in their hundreds across the temple floor. Looking back, I think these snakes were either drugged or had had their fangs removed because no one ever seemed to be bitten. You could have a picture taken with a snake draped around your neck, or buy a dead rat to feed to one of them. I chose not to do either…

While in Singapore I had the time to re-establish my love of Girl Guiding. I hadn't been involved in this for years but to fill some spare time I decided to help out with the Guide company at Changi. The Company comprised mainly of British daughters of serving personnel, and after a while I was asked to take charge of its running because my predecessor's tour of duty was finishing.

I agreed to do this, and with the new job came the responsibility of organising that year's Guide camp at the Padang, a large open playing field in the centre of Singapore. Guide companies came from all over the region – Indian, Chinese, Malay, American, Australian and British – and we even had a company from the local leper colony, with whom we worked quite closely. Of them all, the British Guides were among the most challenging – there were a number of real 'little darlings' among their members!

This was an enormous camp of hundreds of girls and because they were from all nationalities one of the biggest issues was who would eat what, and when. We started off having to plan separately for everyone because, for example, the British mothers didn't want their girls to mix with the Indians, the Indian mothers were terrified of their daughters eating something religiously 'unclean' and the Malay mothers refused to allow any animals near where their girls would eat. So it was a logistical nightmare. Luckily, the army had lent us several huge tents and helped us to put them up, so at least we could have a degree of separation at mealtimes. Plus, because it was so hot we couldn't store anything and every day we had to shop for the food – not easy when you're catering for around 200 girls over the course of a ten-day camp. Anyway, by the end of the get-together the mothers' rules appeared to have broken down because all nationalities were dining with each other and seemingly didn't care about what they were eating. One of the Indian Guides came up to me after one particular lunch and asked me what she'd just had, "because it was delicious!" I hadn't the heart to tell her that it may well have been corned beef. We had a lot of fun together, singing Guide songs around the campfire, playing games and learning new skills. The whole thing was like a military operation and at the end of it, when I took down the flag of Singapore for the last time, I was exhausted and elated.

As ever, all good things come to an end, and after an amazing three-year adventure in Singapore, Ron was to be posted back to England, working at GCHQ in Cheltenham. We'd had a great life but were also looking forward to coming home and experiencing a part of our own country we knew little about. We came home on the passenger liner SS Oronsay and sailed via the tip of Africa because there was some trouble in Egypt at the time, which meant the ship could not safely use the Suez Canal. We stopped in Cape Town and climbed Table Mountain, which thrilled the boys. By this time Colin was 13, Gordon was 10 and Nigel was 5. They'd grown up considerably during their years in Singapore and could appreciate how lucky they were to see the world this way. Ron and I understood this privilege too, and secretly we hoped it wouldn't be too long before a new adventure abroad would begin for us.

CHAPTER 13 – OLIVE JOINS THE ARMY!

During our time in Singapore we'd saved up enough money to buy a house in England, and after a short period renting in the village of Bishops Cleeve, north of Cheltenham, we put the deposit down on a house in Delabere Road. It was the beginning of a long relationship with Gloucestershire and, for a few of us in the family, one that endures to this day.

The house was a newly-built three-bed semi of the type that was springing up on new estates all over the country in the 1960s. The process of buying it was interesting; we could only use a building society that was approved by the Civil Service – this is how bureaucracy worked all those years ago. We went into a local estate agent, Parkers, and a man in there took us out for lunch before we visited the estate and saw the house. We decided to have it when we noticed kids running about the estate and we knew this would be a good place to bring up the boys.

The house is still there, and last time I visited it still had the same door! The children went to school in the area (starting a tradition that has continued with some of my grandchildren and great-grandchildren) and they were very happy. They played cricket and football on the field at the back of the house and I took up Guiding again. The local Methodist church needed a Guide Captain and I volunteered to take over and run the company. The girls were an interesting bunch, a fair few being of the 'horsey' persuasion. At the time, ranks in the Guides were very much based on military lines - Captain, Lieutenant, etc – which was a throwback to the days of Baden Powell. It was decided we could call ourselves something else, so my group chose names related to all things 'horse'. So I became the Lone Ranger and my deputy was Tonto. We attended an annual church parade in Cheltenham and I was hauled over the coals for allowing my girls to modify their skirts into 'minis', which were all the rage then. I was also carpeted because some of them had left chewing gum stuck to the pews of the church. I think they were more St Trinian's than Girl Guides!

At the time we were leaving Singapore we wondered what we might do with Simba, the German Shepherd puppy we'd acquired as a guard dog and a playmate for the boys. We had the thought that we might have to give him to someone else but the boys, especially Nigel, begged us to bring him back and eventually we agreed. Simba travelled to England on a merchant navy ship and was completely spoiled by the crew who adopted him as a kind of mascot. Once in England he had to go into quarantine for six months and although we were able to visit him he grew miserable and thin during his time in doggy jail.

After six months his sentence was up and we brought him back to Delabere Road, to the delight of the boys. However, their happiness wasn't shared by our neighbours. Simba hadn't forgotten he was supposed to be a guard dog and he would regularly get out of the garden and patrol the road. By now he was a big dog and as well as terrorising the neighbours, would go for other dogs in the street. One day he got out and grabbed hold of a small white poodle belonging to an old man. The poor little dog only just survived the encounter and the old man was terribly shaken up. Clearly, Simba was a liability and Ron and I made the awful decision that the best thing would be to have him put to sleep.

However, we couldn't bear to tell the boys the truth. Shamefully, we told them a white lie. Simba, we said, had joined the RAF and was being trained to parachute out of aircraft and do all sorts of amazing things for his Queen and country. The boys thought this was absolutely wonderful, particularly Nigel, who told all his friends how proud he was of his pet in the RAF. When anything ever came on the TV about the air force Nigel would look out for Simba and we'd continue the untruth by telling him he had been promoted. I think Nigel was about 15 when he discovered the truth, and he wasn't very happy! Poor Simba — perhaps he'd have made a good police dog or indeed, an RAF or army dog, but we didn't think about it at the time and just did what we thought was best for everybody. I hope the boys have forgiven us!

We were back for a year or so when Ron got news of his next posting – Hong Kong. That was an exciting piece of news but we had settled so very well into Bishops Cleeve and I was reluctant just to sell up and move on without looking back. I felt we needed a base in the UK so we decided to let the house to an American serviceman who was based nearby, plus his family. When this was all signed and sealed I was happy and so we made our way to Brize Norton and a flight (no long sea voyages by now) to Hong Kong. This time there were only four of us. Colin had elected to go to Wray Castle in Cumbria, by then a training college for cadets who wanted to go into the Merchant Navy as radio officers. It was an interesting building, having been owned in Victorian times by the man who founded the National Trust, and it was also visited by a young Beatrix Potter, who liked the area so much that she later bought Hill Top Farm, close by Wray Castle, and began writing her famous stories there. Colin's ambition to go into the Merchant Navy as a radio officer was very pleasing to Ron and he promised to come out to Hong Kong for his holidays.

Our overnight accommodation at Brize Norton was Officer-class, a novelty for us as we were usually at 'sergeant' standard. Then we climbed aboard the VC-10 and sat with our backs to the cockpit, eating RAF sandwiches and drinking RAF tea. The first stop was Bahrain and I think it was unscheduled as there was a poorly child on board who needed treatment. We landed at the RAF base there and I volunteered to accompany the child and his mother to the station hospital. It was the middle of the night, but still incredibly hot as we got into an ambulance. Anyway, there was nothing seriously wrong with him so he had an injection, returned to the plane and we were off again.

Then we came down in Singapore. Johnnie and Esther were still living here, and we had a couple of hours' spare so we booked a taxi to go and collect whoever was at home so they could meet up with us. All our fellow passengers thought we were mad: "You can't trust such taxi drivers," "You'll never see your money again," etc.

However, the taxi driver had assured us he would deliver, and he was as good as his word. Johnny was at work but Esther turned up and we whiled away a pleasant hour or so in the airport. It's incredible to think that security then was more or less non-existent. You could wander out of the airport, book a taxi, wander back in and have a guest visit you – no one checking bags or passports. These were innocent, carefree days.

Eventually we arrived at Kai Tak airport and coming into land was the most frightening thing I'd ever experienced. The sea looked to be inches away, as did the rooftops and the skyscrapers, all zooming up towards us. How those pilots did it safely, day after day, I'll never know. Our arrival in the Crown Colony (as it was known then) was marked by the most horrendous rainstorm and we were a bit taken aback by the amount of water lashing the streets and buildings. This was a taste of things to come.

We were to be based in the Imperial Hotel at the bottom of Nathan Road, the busiest of all the roads in Kowloon, and it seemed to us that the people of Hong Kong never bothered going to bed. Very quickly we noticed that it was as busy at two o'clock in the morning as at two o'clock in the afternoon. The traffic never stopped and car horns honked endlessly. To be honest, at first it was all a bit of a culture shock but as the rains departed and we began to see the stunning urban beauty of this overcrowded and fascinating place we slowly started to feel at home.

We stayed in the hotel for quite a while. I recall fusing all the lights in the place when I decided to do some ironing one day, and plugged the electric iron into the nearest light socket. Also, Ron decided that we couldn't afford to eat in the hotel restaurant every night and would insist that we buy food from the nearby shops and eat it in our room. He also requested that the hotel bring him a large jug of boiling water each time he wanted to make tea. Well, the hotel quickly got wise to this and one day the woman who brought the hot water asked us what we'd be using it for. At first, Ron wouldn't say but the lady insisted and didn't seem to want to go without receiving an answer. "Oh, alright!" Ron shouted, "it's for washing. I'm going to wash my personal bits! Are you happy now?!" We could hardly look at each other for laughing as the maid scuttled away in embarrassment. Needless to say, they never asked again...

At first, Ron did most of the looking-around for new houses while I kept an eye on the children back at the hotel. He was posted to a listening hut right up on the Chinese border and wanted to find a property not too far from his workplace. One day, he came back with a colleague, who had been escorting him around various properties, and mentioned that he'd been to see a house in the New Territories, a place on Castle Peak Road overlooking the South China Sea. This area was known as the 'Riviera of Hong Kong' and had spectacular views. Ron, however, had other ideas.

"Ah, it wasn't very good, Olive," he said, "so I turned it down."

"On the contrary," his friend piped up, "it was a beautiful place and I think you should go to see it, Olive."

On his advice, Ron and I went back to the house and the man was right – it was a lovely house in an area called Vista Del Mar, complete with an amazing view and a beautiful beach right below us. It really could've been the French Riviera. In other words, it was perfect and we signed up straight away. As in Singapore, we hired an 'amah' who would help with the household chores and the children. Gordon and Nigel were enrolled in army schools and although they had a long journey every day over the notoriously steep and winding Route 'TWISK' (linking Tsuen Wan and Sek Kong) they soon settled in. Our next-door neighbours were a major in the Catering Corps and his wife, a lady from South Shields. Naturally we got on very well. There were several service families nearby, so Nigel and Gordon had plenty of kids to play with in the woods at the back of the houses. There must have been a bit of wildlife around because one day all the power blew out around the area and when the engineers came to fix it, they found that the blackout had been caused by a rare Red Panda that had climbed up the electricity pole and touched the wires at the top! There were also rumours of tigers roaming the area but I think that's all they were – rumours.

Our neighbours included a commander in the US Navy, Bob Stanford, and his wife. His job was to manage leave for the American military personnel who were serving in Vietnam at the time. Looking after 'R&R' ('Rest and Recuperation') was no easy task, as these servicemen would cause mayhem the moment they arrived on the island. Bob's wife was from one of the southern states of the US and I don't think she liked Hong Kong at all. In the summer she'd have the air conditioning on permanently, making her house so cold that she actually switched on her electric blanket before she went to bed each night. And in the winter she'd have the heating on full blast. She was very pale and barely left the house. I think she found the whole Far East experience intimidating.

Bob would sometimes take me to work in a huge Mercedes car, which really put my daily bus journey to shame. He seemed to have a sideline in providing Rolls Royce cars for local hotels, particularly the Peninsular, which prided itself on having the largest fleet of Rolls Royces in the world. No doubt a lot of kumshaw was changing hands! Anyway, Bob would occasionally see if we'd like a ride in a Roller, and we'd all pile in, enjoying the brief experience of complete luxury.

I mentioned about the beautiful beach below our house. Almost all of the time it was beautiful, but there were the occasional days when it was sealed off by the local police. After a while, we got to know what that meant – the discovery of a dead body on the rocks, washed in from mainland China and very often with its arms tied behind its back and signs of torture on the body. This was the time of the Cultural Revolution in China – Chairman Mao and the Little Red Book – and those who disagreed with him regularly met with a terrible end. Amid the splendour and bustling atmosphere of Hong Kong, plus the old-style colonial presence of the British, it was sometimes easy to forget what a huge and powerful neighbour lay just across a narrow border. Though I dare say Ron was far more aware of it than I was, given that he was monitoring Chinese communications for a living.

We made the best of our new circumstances and began to explore our environment. We would cross over on the North Point Ferry and drive on the coastal route to Sek Kong via

Repulse Bay, where we would spend many hours on the beach and in the water. We would arrive at CSOS Little Sai Wan, (Composite Signals Organisation Station), the HQ for GCHQ in Hong Kong, where we would have a meal, go swimming or just watch a cricket match.

We also visited Stonecutter's Island, which had been used as an ammunition dump and was off-limits to anyone not connected with the British military. It had a lovely harbour and an amazing saltwater swimming pool that the boys loved. We didn't go much further to explore the island, however, because the place was said to be full of poisonous snakes. This was a legacy of World War Two, because the invading Japanese had used it as a huge snake farm in which they extracted the venom of various species to use as anti-bite serum in combat zones. When they surrendered they'd abandoned the snakes and they were said to roam free on the island, ready to sink their fangs into the unwary!

With the boys at school, Ron working long hours and unsociable shifts and an amah looking after the domestic stuff, I found myself with a lot of time on my hands. I hadn't worked since our time in Scotland and although I don't recall actively looking for a job while in Hong Kong, perhaps I was subconsciously sensing that I needed a bit more fulfilment than I was getting.

One evening Ron and I were at a dinner party. It was the usual mix of military types and their wives, and as on many of these occasions the chit-chat tended to revolve around the same issues. Anyway, I was talking to a woman who noticed my accent and she asked where I was from. When I told her, she said, "Oh! There's a lady here from Sunderland. I'll introduce you." And with that she brought over a smartly dressed woman about 10 years older than me whose husband was a serving officer.

We got chatting about various places in the North East, and how I was getting on in Hong Kong. After a short while I noticed her really staring at me. She paused, then said, "I hope this doesn't sound silly, but I think I know you. Can I ask you where you worked in Sunderland?"

"Mackenzie and Co," I replied. "The solicitors' in John Street."

"I knew it!" she said. "I never forget a face. I was the young girl who worked with Mr Cope."

Well, my stomach did a somersault. Now I knew her. At the time she was a young secretary who worked with a solicitor called Edward Cope, otherwise known as 'the poor man's lawyer'. When our bomb-damaged office was repaired, a pre-fab was added to the rear of the building and it was out of this makeshift office that Mr Cope and his secretary worked. He would deal with cases involving the poor of Sunderland who had received some kind of financial assistance – perhaps an early version of the Legal Aid scheme – to fight disputes with landlords, employers and the like.

Well, this was some coincidence and the lady and I chatted for a long time about the various characters at Mackenzie and Co. She told me she was working as a secretary to an army colonel based in Victoria Barracks, a part of the British military base on Hong Kong Island. When she described the work it sounded a bit mind-boggling; all military terms, acronyms and army slang. Finally we parted but agreed to keep in touch.

A few weeks later she rang me at home. "You've been on my mind, Olive," she said, "because my husband is being posted home for a few months and I think I'd like to go with him. But I also want to keep my job on. Do you think you'd be interested in taking it over temporarily while I'm away?"

"Oh, I don't know," I replied. "It's been a long time since I did anything like that. I'm not sure I'm really up to it."

"I remember you when you were at Mackenzie and Co, Olive," she replied, "and I know what you're capable of. Believe me, you could do this job standing on your head."

I still wasn't sure, and told her so. But she persisted, telling me that if I changed my mind I could contact someone at Victoria Barracks and come in for a typing test. After I put the phone down I began to think of the possibilities. 'It would be nice to fill my days with something constructive,' I thought, and now that the kids were off my hands and at school, some interesting work might relieve a bit of the boredom I felt had started to creep in.

So I changed my mind, rang the number the lady had given me and went in for the test. Everything went well and it looked like I'd be starting a new career when the lady rang to tell me that the army had changed its mind, her husband wasn't going to be posted home and so she'd be staying at her job. I thought that might be fate, and that I was probably destined not to work again... until I had a call from an army employee at Osborn Barracks, Kowloon, who'd heard about me. He told me that the secretary of Brigadier Harry Illing had gone home and would I be interested in filling the post?

Again, I got a bit of cold feet over this. "I don't know anything about the army," I said, "and I'm not sure I'm the right person for the job." I might have been a bit intimidated too. This Brigadier was the commander at Osborn Barracks and I imagined a fierce military type, barking orders at me while I sat miserably in his office, day after day. I didn't fancy that, so I put the idea out of my mind.

However, later on that evening the phone rang again and this time it was the Brigadier himself. "Look, Mrs Roberts," he said, "I'm in a bit of a fix. I'm only here for another few months and I just need someone to help me for a short while."

"Oh, I think I'd be useless," I replied.

"I'll be honest – you can't be any worse than the lady I've just had. Why don't you pop in and see me?"

Brigadier Illing sounded pleasant enough on the phone and so I agreed to see him. He was a charming man and seemed keen to take me on. But there was one stipulation on my part – that I would be leaving every day in order to get home on time for the boys arriving from school. The Brigadier agreed without any fuss; it was obvious he needed some help, and quickly.

As I said, I knew nothing about the army but Brigadier Illing was a good teacher. And so he should be… he was a D-Day veteran who'd won the Military Cross twice during the Second World War and he was a soldier through and through. He was a nice man, but he could be funny sometimes in that he liked everything just so. If you knew what he wanted and you did it to his satisfaction, he was absolutely fine.

He was patient when it came to passing on his army knowledge to me. The number of acronyms for this and that were mind-boggling. I knew what GCHQ stood for, obviously, but for anything else I was stumped. One of the very first things I took down in dictation from the Brigadier included the acronym 'MoD'. I had some idea this was to do with the army, so I wrote it in full as 'Modern Army'. When Brigadier Illing eventually saw it he patiently explained that while our army was indeed modern, 'MoD' actually stood for Ministry of Defence! Well, there was only one way to go from there and that was up….

To get to work I needed to catch a minibus which would take me down from where I was living to the barracks. The buses were set up by a British official of the Hong Kong government and it seemed to be a way of getting hundreds of taxis off the road, to be replaced by these nine-seater vehicles that would stop anywhere. Travelling in them was an interesting experience. You'd be sat next to local people taking poultry and eggs to market, along with other British people going to work. And it's no exaggeration to say that these buses were jerry-built. After a few months their floors almost completely rusted away, and you were left with the terrifying experience of seeing your legs dangling above white lines speeding past! There were a lot of complaints about them, and no wonder.

In August 1971 Hong Kong was devastated by Typhoon Rose, which made landfall on the island. It was the worst storm of its kind for ten years and the eye of it came directly over our house. I must admit to being terrified as the wind roared overhead, and for good reason, too; the devastation it caused was huge, with the loss of life running into the hundreds. The build-up to it was frightening enough. We were all aware it was coming and each day the forecasters told us it was becoming stronger and stronger. Our amah, who was living on a fish farm at the time with her husband, moved in with us because she was fearful her small house would be blown away. We barricaded ourselves in one room and battened down the hatches as the typhoon hit. The house shook, the wind howled through every crack, and water was coming in through the walls. The side of our garage blew down, but other than that we were safe. Unfortunately not everyone was so lucky. At the time, gambling was forbidden in Hong Kong (except at the racecourse) and anyone wanting to gamble had to take a special ferry into open waters, where the rules didn't apply. The Chinese are famously obsessive gamblers and even in the midst of a typhoon hundreds of them insisted on piling aboard one such ferry, the 'Fat San', going between Hong Kong and Macau. Quickly the boat got into trouble and we had a grandstand view of the whole horrible experience from our window. We could see it plunging down into the boiling sea before being tossed up again a few minutes later. Ron rang the coastguard to let them know that the ferry was in trouble, but even then it was probably too late. Eventually it capsized, with a large loss of life.

After the typhoon passed we ventured out and saw the destruction for ourselves. Boats had been thrown up on to roads and the shanty villages which sprang up regularly had simply been blown away. Many people were killed, and many more made homeless. It was an awful thing to happen to the island, and it's stuck in the mind of those of us who experienced those terrifying, yet exhilarating few days.

It was during this tour that Uncle Peter, the roguish character who was married to Auntie Bella, came out to visit us. He'd barely been out of the North East so he was flabbergasted by all the modernity of Hong Kong. For example, he'd never experienced a multi-storey car park before. He was in the passenger seat, with Ron driving, and as we looked for a space he was saying, "Ron, you bugger, we've been round here once, why are we going around again?" He had no idea that we were going upwards!

He also had what I might call a British sense of humour that doesn't always go down well when abroad. He had no inhibitions about calling Chinese taxi drivers various unflattering names, and I just hoped they didn't understand his Geordie accent – though I was aware just how many Chinese spoke good English.

Uncle Peter wasn't much bothered about sightseeing. His idea of a good time was to sit on our balcony with the South China Morning Post and watch the ships passing by. The paper detailed all the shipping movements of the day, so Peter delighted in telling us which ship had arrived, what it was carrying, tonnage etc. And while he watched the flotilla, he would drink – just about everything we had in the house! He even drank a large bottle of Chinese rice wine, sealed at its neck with red wax, which was actually an ornament. This drove our amah mad, who reported that he was paralytic most of the time.

We introduced him to groups of soldiers we knew at Osborn Barracks. They could spot a fellow rascal and decided to take him under their collective wing. He was invited to the Sergeants' Mess and presented with a bottle or two of his favourite whisky, Johnnie Walker's Black Label. He enjoyed a few games of bowls and darts and then they took him for a meal and to meet all the ladies. When he returned home he was as drunk as a lord and Ron had to completely undress him then put him to bed. But he'd had a fantastic time. The following day a whole load of army surplus – socks, pullovers, ties and the like – were left on my desk at work as a present for him. When he arrived home to East Boldon he bragged so much about his experiences that local people would hide when they saw him coming down the street.

I like meeting people and I am a talker, so it was no surprise when I fell into a conversation with a Hong Kong Chinese lady I met in hospital. I wasn't ill – I'd taken my amah there, who was feeling poorly and couldn't afford treatment. So I took her to a hospital run by American Christian missionaries and stayed with her.

While she was being treated I struck up a conversation with this lady in the next bed. She could speak excellent English and seemed to think I was the angel of god for helping out my amah! Well, we chatted for a long time and when my amah recovered she invited the lady to come to visit us.

It turned out she ran a market stall, or maybe a series of market stalls, and whenever she visited (which was frequently) she brought presents of all sorts of things, including dolls that the boys weren't at all interested in and flip-flops made for small Chinese feet which wouldn't go anywhere near fitting my size 8s. I think she just felt bringing a gift was the right thing to do.

By and by, she invited us to come and visit her, warning us that it was a long way up a certain road. She was very keen for us to see her property, which included a fish farm. It turned out she bred tropical fish and sold them all over the world. Ron looked at the map and he was somewhat dubious about this lady's location, as it seemed to be very close to the Chinese border. Ron would've got into terrible trouble had he been caught by the Chinese in this area. Nevertheless, the lady was insistent and we felt we had to go, so off we went and yes, it was a long way along what I think was the area known as Lo Wu Road, in Hong Kong's New Territories. People used to escape Red China by swimming and often landed up here. It was heavily guarded but somehow we managed – either by accident or design – to miss the guards and we walked on and on down this road until we arrived at our friend's house. It smelled to high heaven of fish and there were huge mosquitoes all over the place, along with huge spiders. I'm not a fan of spiders, large or small, so I wasn't happy when I saw these great things dangling down.

She made us welcome and we stayed for a while out of politeness. Ron was very worried that we'd come so far into unknown territory, so eventually we made our excuses and left. Good job we were never caught. I dread to think where we might have ended up!

During this time I picked up my lifelong interest in Guiding once again. I worked with a Guide company in Sek Kong for a while, on an RAF base very close to the Chinese border. This was fine, but when I started working I realised I'd perhaps taken a bit too much on, what with the children and Ron's shifts, so I decided to pack it in. The upshot of this resignation was that I got a letter from Guiding HQ in London, thanking me for all I'd done in Hong Kong – and would I like to take on the role of being the District Commissioner for Girl Guiding in the New Territories? It wasn't as taxing as it sounded; in fact, it was more or less a ceremonial role that involved visiting Guide companies and officiating at ceremonies. So I agreed on that basis and enjoyed the experience of meeting people that it offered.

After 18 months, Brigadier Illing left for the UK and I was left wondering what my future might be now he'd gone. I needn't have worried, because there was another Brigadier arriving and I was asked to stay on. I umm'd and ahh'd a bit but it really didn't take much to convince me to stay. Under Brigadier Illing I'd learned quite a bit about the army and I was enjoying hearing all the comings and goings of life at the top of the military tree. It wasn't secret work but some of it was confidential and now I had an inkling of how Ron viewed his own role as a 'listener-in'. When Brigadier Illing left, he wrote me a nice reference, which read:

"This lady has been my PA for the last eighteen months. She has been a most pleasant, helpful and cooperative person to deal with, thoroughly reliable and trustworthy. She has a well-balanced and sensible outlook and in her dealings with others has always displayed common sense and tact. She is a good shorthand/typist and her work has throughout been most satisfactory. It has been a pleasure working with this lady and I am happy to give her an excellent reference."

Well, I was most flattered. You don't get that kind of treatment in civilian life! And of course, those reading this story who know me will agree with every single word…!

The new Brigadier was a man named Peter Prescott and, unlike his predecessor, who was Infantry, the new commander was from the Brigade of Guards. And he'd been to Eton. Cue a huge amount of preparation for his arrival, including the typical military habit of scrubbing and polishing everything that didn't move – and everything that did move too. The whole barracks received a top-to-bottom smarten-up and on the day he arrived we all stood to attention as he greeted us warmly.

From the start, I liked Brigadier Prescott. He also had won a Military Cross while serving in World War Two with the Grenadier Guards, and he was a lovely man, tall and handsome with a very pleasant wife. He hadn't been in Hong Kong before, having previously commanded the Grenadier Guards in West Germany, so he relied quite heavily on me as his PA while he found his feet. My job was to take all the minutes and memos, type them up, arrange the daily diary, plan visits to HQ, sort out transport and book in vehicles on the Kowloon Ferry.

This latter part of my job could be quite complicated, especially if the traffic was bad or there was some delay getting on or off the ferry. Brigadier Illing didn't mind waiting in the staff car should he find himself early for a meeting at HQ but Brigadier Prescott was a different matter. The first time it happened he was waiting for about 30 minutes in all his regalia and he was not best pleased when he returned to barracks. "I don't mind being late," he said to me, "because I went to Eton with them all and they don't mind that. But I don't like waiting around." I accepted his very mild rebuke and made sure that he was almost always bang on time for meetings – and if he was late, that wasn't my problem.

After three years our tour in Hong Kong came to an end and we would be going home to Bishops Cleeve. Ron and I had truly loved the place and I'd got a new lease of life in an interesting job I thoroughly enjoyed and found stimulating. I received another lovely reference, this time from Brigadier Prescott, who wrote:

"Mrs Roberts's duties have included shorthand and typing for myself and other staff officers in my Headquarters to a very high degree of speed and accuracy, the drafting of letters from brief outline given by me, the typing and handling of classified and In Confidence material, filing and registration, accounting for postage, the maintenance of my diary and arrangements for transport including helicopter schedules and social secretary to myself and my wife.

"She has carried out all these duties to my complete satisfaction with an outstanding degree of initiative, common sense, loyalty, good humour and ability.

"She is a highly skilled shorthand typist, has a thoroughly responsible attitude towards security and confidential matters, is hard working, polite, even tempered and a most charming companion. I recommend her most strongly to any employer as Personal Assistant."

And no, if you're wondering, he didn't tell me to 'just make it up'!

A friend of mine took over the PA's job, and after a fabulous few years we flew back to England and life in Bishops Cleeve. We decided not to include Timmy, the cat we'd adopted early in the tour, and which had gone on to have several litters of kittens. This time, we were upfront with the boys about having her put down. She definitely didn't join the RAF! We had to take this course of action, as no one seemed to want her and we didn't like the thought of her going hungry and feral.

By this time Gordon had left Hong Kong and was attending Dean Close, a private school in Cheltenham where he would meet his future wife, Lynn. She was an American student whose father was in charge of American personnel working at GCHQ. I'm not sure how happy Gordon and Lynn were at the school, which is perhaps what brought them together.

I had been so pleased to be working for a living again that I thought I'd do a 'TOPS' course (Training Opportunities Scheme) which was set up by the Manpower Services Commission and was designed to offer some training in various occupations to those unemployed or who hadn't been in work for one reason or another (which applied mainly to married women who'd had children). You got a small allowance for going on such a course, plus a daily meal voucher for Woolworths.

The TOPS courses were very much for beginners and I was hoping simply to brush up my skills so that I was able to find a job locally. I didn't tell them I had experience in shorthand and typing, pretending that I was just a beginner too. This was quite easy to pull off in the typing class because I'd just type at the same speed as the others. The shorthand class, however, was a different matter. As you may remember, I'd had an outstanding teacher in the Reverend Hutler at the Thornhill Commercial College in Sunderland. I was good back then and as every shorthand writer knows, you may slow down if you don't practise it but you will never forget it.

So after a while I began to see that the lady teaching us was making a few mistakes. As time went on this seemed to be increasing in frequency. 'These poor people will never learn a thing from her,' I thought, 'because she doesn't seem to know what she's teaching.' Still I didn't say anything until one day when I was having lunch with another course attendee. We were talking about the class and I knew this other woman had some skill in shorthand. So as casually as I could, I said, "Do you think we're being taught properly here?"

The woman's eyes opened wide. "No," she said, shocked, "I don't think we are."

I nodded. "You can do shorthand quite well, can't you?" I said. The woman admitted that she could, so I told her about my experience. We agreed that this wouldn't do, so we went to see the head person (who could also do shorthand) and she agreed she'd sit in on a lesson, which she did – and she was horrified.

After this, the head lady realised that my colleague and I were better at shorthand than anyone suspected, so she put us in a class of our own and together we worked on upping our speeds. Which was far more useful than learning Pitman's completely the wrong way.

It was nice being around a bunch of girls again, and even though I was in my early 40s by this time I decided to throw caution to the wind and start wearing a mini skirt which were all the rage then. And I enjoyed it too – I was in my element. I passed the TOPS course and officially increased my shorthand speed to 120 words a minute during a Pitman's examination. I started to apply for jobs and after a couple of short spells with an estate agency and a charity, I got a job with the regional hospital board as secretary to the treasurer. And I hated it from the first minute I got there. The hospital board was involved in the planning for a new hospital but I never saw the treasurer unless he was giving me dictation. Unlike the army officers I'd worked for, who operated on a far more personal level, there was little to no contact between me and this man. Not only that, but there seemed to be a real 'atmosphere' of unpleasantness around the place and after a month I handed in my notice. I had to work another month's notice period but I gritted my teeth, got through it, then on the final day skipped out of there like Morecambe and Wise!

By now, Colin had left school and was working at Smiths Industries in Cheltenham, which made instruments and mechanisms for a range of industries including nautical, aeronautical, automotive, medical etc. He had also met his wife-to-be, Sybil, and we were lucky enough to be able to celebrate their wedding during the period we were based in the UK. They were married at Shurdington Parish Church on a beautiful hot summer's day, and after the wedding we had a lovely party at home with all our friends and relatives. It was a great occasion; Sybil looked beautiful and Colin very handsome.

Very soon after this we were given news of Ron's new posting, and to our delight it would be back to Hong Kong, but not in the New Territories – this time we would be on Hong Kong Island. Nigel didn't want to go to boarding school so he elected to come back out with us. Colin and Sybil decided to take on the running of the house in Bishops Cleeve and would stay there until we came back after three years. And so began a new chapter of our adventures, in a place we knew and loved, but wanted to get to know even better.

1. Colin with our dog Zimba.
2. Ron and Colin fishing.
3. David and Margaret Watson, with me and Ron at the Singapura Hotel.

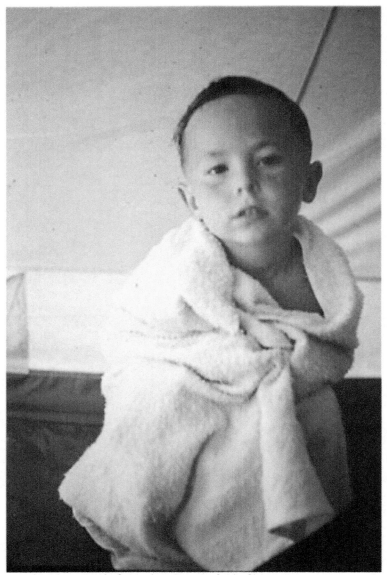

Nigel wrapped up in a towel after swimming, aged 4 in Singapore.

1. Nigel all dressed up in his birthday outfit after his 4th birthday
2. Gordon, Nigel and Colin in the Cameron Highlands in Malaysia.
3. A Spitfire outside Changi Camp in Singapore.
4. Gordon, Colin and Nigel with the 'popsie man' at our first bungalow in Singapore in 1963.
5. Nigel inspecting shells on the beach.

1. Nigel with Zimba. Our next-door neighbour was the Singapore agent for Ovaltine!

2. Gordon jumping from the high board at the Singapore Swimming Club.

3. Nigel's first day at school when he was 4. Our next-door neighbour Jacqueline and her mother Mrs Ee. We all dressed up for the occasion and Mrs Ee wore the Sarong Kebaya.

4. Nigel and Sandra. The boys never wore shirts or shoes if they could help it!

5. Nigel helping with varnishing the baskets again!

1. In Hong Kong around 1969 on the Governor's launch on a day out sailing around the islands.
2. Ron's 'Mam' Jane came to visit us in 1974, here we are at the Royal Hong Kong Yacht Club.
3. Nigel standing overlooking Little Sai Wan – the GCHQ listening base in Hong Kong where Ron worked during our second tour.
4. My Uncle Peter, who is on the front cover of this book, came to visit us in Hong Kong when we lived in the New Territories during our first tour, taken at the Star Ferry in about 1971.
5. Nigel and me at the British Cemetery in Macau; we made friends with the local children and their pet dog!
6. Me taken in the corridors of the Court of Final Appeal in Hong Kong's Statue Square.

1. Colin and Sybil's wedding.
2. Rita, me and my long-lost sister Eleanor.
3. My old friends Muriel Pendlington and Doreen Joliffe (on far left and far right), with Ron's mum Jane and me at Colin and Sybil's wedding.
4. Ron and me cutting a cake before we left for Hong Kong for our second tour in 1973.
5. My first grandchildren Andrew and Helen! Colin and Sybil's children.

1. Bella (Nigel's then girlfriend) when she came to see us in Shotley Bridge after Ron retired.
2. Bella, Ron and me.
3. Ron with Catherine and Maiya (Nigel and Bella's children).
4. Me with Ron and Bella at the house that Nigel and Bella built in Malmesbury.
5. Bell, Ron and Catherine.
6. Megan (Gordon's daughter) with Catherine and Maiya.
7. Luke (Maiya's twin brother) with me and Catherine.

1. Philip (Gordon and Lynn's son) with Luke.
2. Catherine and Nigel, Megan and Maiya, Lynn (Gordon's wife), Bella with Luke sleeping on her shoulder, Philip and Ron, and me with Gordon.
3. Ron and Philip.

1. Bella, Nigel and Maiya, Jenny (Andrew's wife), Helen, Andrew, Sybil, Catherine and Colin.
2. Me, with Ron and my grown-up sons, Nigel, Gordon and Colin.

1. Ron and me, this photo was taken by the newspapers when we were campaigning about Macular Degeneration.
2. Luke, Catherine, Maiya and Helen.
3. Helen, Andrew, Luke, Catherine and Maiya with Grandpa's tree!
4. Luke, Megan and Maiya.
5. We planted a tree and scattered Ron's ashes under it after he died. Here with Lynn and Gordon.

1. Helen and her husband John, Sybil and Colin and me.
2. Maiya and me.
3. Me with Andrew and Helen at Andrew's wedding in the Caribbean.

1. All together at Helen and John's wedding. Maiya and Catherine were bridesmaids, Luke was a page boy.
2. Helen, Bella and me enjoying a glass of wine!
3. Helen, my first grandchild and me!
4. Most of the family together – we went to Hong Kong for my 80th birthday!
5. Nigel and Colin with Andrew at his wedding.

Bella and me at the Tower of London with the poppies marking the centenary of the outbreak of the first world war.

1 Catherine, me and Bella in Monte Carlo.
2. Bella and me enjoying an ice-cream in Rome.
3. Catherine Maiya and me – always with a glass of wine!

1. Me with Polly Anna and Alex and baby Alfie – three of my great grandchildren
2. Bella and me with Alana – my great granddaughter in America.
3. Here I am with Andrew and my great granddaughter Polly-Anna.

1. Me with Polly Anna and Alex and baby Alfie – three of my great grandchildren.
2. My great grandchildren Alfie, Alex and Polly Anna

1. Philip Megan and Gordon with me
2. Alana with her GG (Great Grandma - that's me!!)
3. Megan and Philip with me and Gordon

1. Bella and me at the Garden Party at Buckingham Palace
2. With the Gurkhas at Buckingham Palace
3. Me with Grandpa's tree. Maiya and Catherine both used to say that they remember Grandpa before he became a tree!
4. Catherine and me in Monte Carlo.

My boys, photos taken about 50 years apart. They have not changed a bit!

My final picture. These photos are about 90 years apart – and I still have the same hair style!

CHAPTER 14 – HOME, AND AWAY AGAIN

R on was to be stationed at Little Sai Wan, which was then an RAF signals intelligence base to the east of Hong Kong Island, so it made sense to be based relatively close by. For the first few weeks we took up residence in a hotel overlooking the Happy Valley Racecourse before finding a flat on the 18th floor of a block along the Tai Hang Road.

This was near to Causeway Bay, one of the biggest shopping and leisure centres on the Island. We had the most glorious view over Hong Kong harbour to Kowloon and the airport at Kai Tak. We used to be able to sit on our veranda and watch the planes arriving and leaving. Nigel was attending St George's, a British Army School on Kowloon side, and therefore had a long bus and ferry journey to face every day. Yet he loved it and to this day Hong Kong feels like our second home.

Nigel had become very interested in Subbuteo, the football game that so many boys of that era played, and was at it all day long. He'd read in the Guinness Book of Records that the longest-ever Subbuteo game played continually was seven days, and he became very keen on breaking this world record. So, with a team of five other boys, he approached his school's headmaster and asked him if they could undertake the challenge. Surprisingly, perhaps, the headmaster agreed and the boys decided to play solidly for ten days. Teachers and parents were heavily involved in this challenge, as it would mean the players being fed regularly and bedding down for the night in the school.

The team played 24 hours a day, each person playing for two hours then taking four off. They were fundraising for a local charity and I was interviewed on the radio as part of the money-raising campaign. Someone I knew quite well heard it and told me they didn't realise I was a Geordie until they'd listened to me on the radio! The local English language TV station 'Pearl' came down there quite frequently too. Anyway, they did beat the record and they were justifiably very pleased with their efforts. Sadly, just three weeks later a team from South Africa set a new record, which meant the lads never actually made it into the Guinness Book of Records. Even so, theirs was a remarkable achievement.

Having enjoyed the experience of working for the army I was keen to do it again. I rang a local employment bureau which dealt with such positions and to my amazement I was told that my old job was free because the present occupier of the post was going home. I couldn't believe my luck, but there was one problem – now we were based on Hong Kong Island I would have to take the ferry over to Osborn Barracks.

I thought about it and decided that it was worth the effort. Besides, if Nigel could do it every day without complaint, so could I. By this time Brigadier Prescott had gone home and my new boss would be Brigadier Peter Sibbald. He was Commander of the 51st Gurkha Infantry Brigade and, like my previous army bosses, was unfailingly nice, polite and kind. It was a joy to be back in my old job and it felt as though I'd never been away.

During my previous stay in Hong Kong I'd met many high-ranking army officers, including Major-General Edward John

Sidney Burnett, known to everyone as 'Bunny'. He was commander of the 10th Gurkha Rifles and a decorated veteran of World War Two and campaigns in Malaya and Borneo, among others. Bunny was based at Victoria Barracks on Hong Kong Island but would occasionally visit his soldiers in other parts of the Colony for inspection.

It was during one of these visits to Osborn Barracks that he spotted me working away at my old job. He remembered me, and after greeting me enthusiastically asked what I was up to now.

"Well," I said, "I'm working back here but now I'm travelling in on the ferry."

He smiled. "That's interesting," he said, "because I could really do with someone like you at HQ."

Brigadier Sibbald, who was standing by his side, looked alarmed. "With respect, Sir," he said, "I can't have you poaching my staff. I need Olive here. She's a treasure."

The Major-General shook his head. "I'm afraid not," he said. "You'll just have to find someone else or do without her. If Mrs Roberts wants the job with me, she's got it."

I didn't say anything at that moment, because the look on Brigadier Sibbald's face was enough. There was, however, little he could do about it. It was a gentle order, but an order all the same, and although I liked Brigadier Sibbald very much I was more than happy not to have to do the daily commute over the water.

So off I went and spent an interesting time at HQ working for Bunny, who as well as being the Gurkhas' commander was also Deputy Commander Land Forces. Quickly I was thrown into the situation of coping with Aides-de-camp (ADCs – officers who serve as personal assistants of high-ranking officers) and senior officers from Colonels down. Compared to my previous job at Brigade level, mine was a role that involved dealing with the complex issues that arose at HQ day after day. Luckily, the structure and the military jargon was the same, and somehow I managed to learn to duck and weave as well as anyone else there. After a month or two of settling in (and occasionally wishing I'd never seen the place) I found that I was holding my own and even scoring one or two points over the adversaries who seemed determined to knock you back when they felt you were getting somewhere. But like every Army job people move on and when you're a civilian you stay put longer – and see the back of all the crackpots!

Our spare time was spent socialising with the many friends we'd made during our two tours. Ron was a very keen amateur photographer and was instrumental in setting up various camera clubs in which he and his fellow photographers could go off, take their pictures and print them in their own darkroom. Sunday was the amah's day off so we'd either socialise, play cricket or take out the boat. We didn't have one on the first tour of Hong Kong but during this tour Ron decided to buy an Enterprise sailing dinghy. As in Singapore he spent many hours restoring the boat to its former glory but we didn't spend anywhere near as much time on the water in it because the shipping lanes around the island were so busy. We were members of the Royal Hong Kong Yacht Club, one of the world's most prestigious, and even if we weren't sailing from it much, we certainly enjoyed its luxurious facilities.

Ron's mother came out to visit us during this time. She had a slipped disc and had to wear a surgical corset. Somehow or other, the security people at whatever Arab country they landed in en route seemed very interested in this device.

"Oh, Olive," she said, "they were poking and prodding me. And the man looked like a sheikh. He's all the sheikh's robes. And there was a woman there who looked like his wife."

"Maybe he was a sheikh?" I suggested.

"Well, I don't know if he was or he wasn't," she said, still seemingly in shock, "but he didn't half look like one. And he was fascinated by this corset."

Well, Lord only knows what had gone on but she'd arrived safely enough and was really enjoying what Hong Kong had to offer. A little too much, perhaps, because she tucked into a lot of sweet things and it was only when she started to have a bit of an episode did we realise she had diabetes.

We took her to the British Military Hospital, where the medical staff were delighted to see her. "We don't get many grandmas here," said one of the medical officers. "It's all squaddies." So she received first-class treatment and was given a variety of tests that I don't think she'd have had in a standard UK NHS hospital.

I think she was bemused, or possibly confused, by it all. One day, a catering officer came to her bedside and asked her what she'd like to eat. "Not very much," she replied, "because I've not been feeling very well."

"Oh, that's a shame," he replied, "but what can we tempt you with?"

"I've got to keep off the treats," she said, "but I must say – it's very unusual for a doctor to stand at the end of my bed and ask me what I'd like for dinner. That wouldn't happen in England, because they always tell me what I CAN'T eat."

The catering officer laughed heartily at this, and explained that he wasn't a doctor – no matter how much he might have looked like one to Ron's mother!

She stayed for two months and went home with a sheaf of papers from the hospital which she presented to her own GP. Needless to say, she didn't get anywhere near the same level of care but as it turned out she'd only had a kidney infection anyway, so there wasn't much cause for alarm.

I got on very well with the Chinese people, and worked with many of them. They were hard-working and clever. I remember one man who was particularly bright but wasn't given a good report of his work by his British boss because 'we wouldn't want to lose him.' In other words they were holding him back from promotion, which I thought was most unfair. Really, a lot of them should've been running their own businesses instead of working for the British Army, but they could also see the salary and pension benefits, plus access to good schools for their children. They put a lot of store on education and they all spoke great English. I did try my best with a bit of Cantonese, but only a word or a phrase here and there.

General Bunny retired while I was working for him. His plan was to move to Australia and develop a salmon farm in the Blue Mountains, but this didn't come off due to illness. However, I helped to pack all his belongings and sort out all his schedules. He was to be replaced by Major-General Ronald William Lorne McAlister, better known as 'Ronnie'. He too was Gurkha Rifles and when he arrived he took command of the Brigade of Gurkhas as well as becoming Deputy Commander Land Forces. When he arrived he walked straight into the office and said, "Which one is mine, then?" When I said it was me, he immediately focused on getting to know me, and of all the military men I'd worked for, I think it was General McAlister I liked the best. It didn't matter who you were, what your background was or where you came from, Ronnie was simply interested in you as a person, and not just as a cog in the British Army machine.

He was an intellectual man who liked reading and writing. In many ways he was more like a professor than a soldier. But he'd certainly earned his stripes. As a young man he'd been commissioned into the Indian Army then fought the Japanese in Burma. After the war he went on to serve in Malaya and Borneo. He'd previously served in Hong Kong and at one stage in the late 1960s had helped to put down an armed Communist revolt that might have led to a full-scale invasion of Hong Kong by the Chinese. He was also kidnapped by Chinese soldiers and it was feared he might be taken to China, before he was eventually released unharmed.

Ronnie was an affable man, as was his Gurkha ADC Nima Wangdi Lama, and my working life once again took on a rosy glow. I found that I could achieve most of the aims of the job and more – taking on a fair amount of the ADC's work as well – and I enjoyed all the challenges. There were many differences between HQ and Osborn Barracks but I soon discovered that if I was stuck, I could ring up various contacts I'd made for advice. A typical working day for General Ronnie would involve me coming in before he did and opening the safe, which only I had access to. This is where the orders and secret documents were kept, and I would recover from inside whatever was necessary for the day ahead. When he arrived I'd get him some coffee and we'd go through all the correspondence, locally and from abroad. It was during one of these letter-opening sessions that we learned he'd received the Order of the Bath.

I got to know Nima very well. Compared to one or two other ADCs I'd met, he was a pleasure to be around. I recall working with one ADC from the Guards, who laughed heartily when I said my father had been in the Cycling Corps during World War One. He couldn't believe such a unit had existed, and he told me so. I was annoyed, telling this man that my father had spent years in the trenches. That quietened him down, and I didn't speak to him much after that. In contrast, Nima considered me to be a fully-fledged member of the Gurkha family. Whenever there was a social or formal occasion involving the Gurkhas, he made sure Ron and I were invited. We couldn't go to everything, and nor did I want to because we needed family time too, but it was lovely to occasionally visit the Governor's yacht with Ron, watch the racing at Happy Valley or attend a Regimental dinner. I got to know many Gurkhas during this period and I thought they were lovely people, although I was warned by General Ronnie not to attend one event I'd been invited to; a gathering to celebrate the Hindu festival of Dashain. He described the ritual beheading of a number of goats by Gurkhas using their famous curved kukri knives. "It can get rather messy, Olive," he said with typical understatement, "so it's probably best to turn that one down." So I did, and I'm glad.

To quickly jump forward many years, I attended the Queen's Garden Party in 2018 and at one point during the afternoon I spotted two men whom I knew were 10th Gurkha Rifles because of their uniforms. I stopped them for a chat and of course they'd heard of General McAlister. I told them a bit about my time in Hong Kong with the Gurkhas and I think they were amazed that an elderly lady knew so much about them!

I helped General Ronnie to write a history of the 10th Gurkha Rifles. He would put everything down in longhand and it was my job to type it up. Mostly I'd do this in my own time and on my own portable typewriter. Very often I'd go into the office at a weekend or when the General was away, as he didn't like the sound of the typewriter keys clattering all through the working day. When I went in to do this work I'd always go dressed casually, a pair of jeans perhaps, or trousers. For 'proper' work I'd usually wear a skirt and heels. One day I came out of HQ and was just having a chat with a colleague before heading home when I was approached by a female army officer.

"I've been watching you," she said tetchily, "and I thought I'd let you know that you shouldn't wear trousers to work. I tell all my office staff they must wear their nice things for work, and keep trousers and the like for outside activities."

I was taken aback by this officer's attitude. She was treating me like a private soldier, so I pointed out that actually I was a civilian, and that I was outside working hours.

"That may be," she replied, "but I'm just putting you right."

She marched off and I went home with this sharp little exchange running through my mind. I wondered if someone higher up had ordered her to say all this to me, and as I spoke to

Ron I knew I was fretting about it.

"If you think the General is behind it, then just ask him when he's next in," said Ron. He usually had a simple solution to the problem and the following Monday morning, when the General walked through the office door, I took a deep breath and asked if he'd ordered the female officer to tick me off.

"Goodness me, of course not," he said. "My wife wears trousers all the time. Olive, as long as you do your work you can wear exactly what you want to wear."

I was pleased to hear this, but I knew the female officer worked downstairs and that I would definitely encounter her again. I told the General this.

"I'll tell you what to do," he said. "Go down to where she works, open the door and simply say that I've told you that you can wear what you like."

So I went down and knocked on her door. She gave me permission to enter but before she could speak I said, "About the trousers... I've mentioned the situation to General McAlister and he says it's OK." She looked all flustered and without another word I turned on my heel and walked out, closing the door rather firmly behind me. Later that day I was walking up Garden Lane to a little café run by two old English ladies who served up staple British food like beans on toast. As I approached the café I heard footsteps behind me and a voice shouting, "Excuse me! Excuse me!" I turned around and it was the female officer. I ignored her, walked on and eventually lost her. A day or so later I encountered her again as I was leaving the Hong Kong Yacht Club with General McAlister and Ron. She was just on her way in and she looked at me as if to say, 'Who the hell is she?' But she didn't say a word and never again was I ticked off for what I should or shouldn't be wearing.

We all knew that time in Hong Kong was limited, and not just from a personal point of view. Under the terms of a long-standing agreement, the Colony would be handed over to the Chinese in 1997 and even in 1977, when we were there, preparations were beginning to put this historic plan into action. We started to see military posts being cut back and more high-ranking civil service people being brought in to run Hong Kong. It was agreed by all sides that the handover should be as smooth and amicable as possible and this would take a lot of time, a lot of discussion and a lot of meetings. I attended many of these, often going on late into the night, where every aspect of the handover and the logistics of how Hong Kong would be run after 1997 were discussed. These meetings were held in secret – no Chinese people were allowed to attend for fear there may be Communist spies among their number, so it was up to me and another trusted secretary to take the minutes and type up everything as soon as possible.

Eventually General McAlister learned that he was to be posted home. I knew that Ron and I, having done our three years, wouldn't be far behind him, and I decided that when the General left I would follow him out and not do any more work for the army. It was a hard decision to make, as I had thoroughly enjoyed my time in this role, but I was also aware that things were changing quickly in Hong Kong and I wanted to leave with only good memories.

As ever, my boss wrote me a lovely testimonial:

"Mrs Olive Roberts has been my PA for just over two years. It has been a great pleasure working for a first-class stenographer/typist and someone so naturally charming, tactful and thoughtful as a person. She really seems to have enjoyed making my administrative and social arrangements and I have also trusted her implicitly with all manner of personal correspondence.

"Much as I have appreciated her excellent work in the office, her greatest impact has, in fact, been felt outside. So many people have told me what a pleasure it is to ring Mrs Roberts, or be rung by her and to find her ever cheerful, helpful, cooperative, well-mannered and efficient. All this has, of course, reflected on me and I am grateful.

"I strongly recommend Mrs Roberts as PA to a senior officer, government official or businessman."

General Ronnie was also kind enough to send me a handwritten thank-you note after Ron and I presented him with some crystal glasses. He said:

"My dear Olive, Thank you so much for the delightful glasses you gave me and for the very kind letter that came with them.

"I am not good at saying goodbye so I could not thank you adequately for all your help and support over the happy years. I could not have asked for anyone nicer or more efficient to work with – I basked in your reflected personality!

"With very best wishes for the future. Love and thanks from Sally too.

"Ronnie."

As he mentioned, he wasn't good at saying 'goodbye' but it would've been bad form for him to have left without some kind of get-together, so he planned 'just a little gathering' with army officers and close friends. Of course, Ronnie being Ronnie he invited everyone, so that an intimate lunchtime occasion had now become a full-blown drinks party. We had nowhere near enough glasses so the General told me to go into the officers' mess and get as many as we needed. Even though I'd officially finished it seemed I was still on duty! Anyway, I was presented with a lovely pendant on behalf of the 10th Gurkhas and I felt myself very lucky to have done this job and met so many wonderful people as a result of it.

As I've said, Hong Kong is still a special place for me, and for Nigel too, I think, as he spent so many years growing up there. Going back there always feels like home and in many ways I think it has changed for the better. For a start I don't think corruption is as rife as it was then, and while I'm sure the older citizens of Hong Kong preferred being under British rule, the generation since 1997 have no memories of the British now.

Ron and I celebrated our Silver Wedding on the island. This coincided with a visit from Colin and Sybil who bought us some lovely wine glasses that I treasure to this day. We sent them home on the plane, and just a few short years later we were heading back to England ourselves. Cheltenham would be our first stop, but only to sell the house in Bishops Cleeve because Ron had been posted to a former RAF station near Taunton, Somerset, where there was now a signals research station. In fact, we sold the house to Margaret (my cousin) and her husband David, who had now left the RAF. They had young children and so our family-focused house was very suitable for them.

I should mention that we brought a budgie home from Hong Kong. We'd bought it for Nigel and christened it Kiki. The bird became very tame, and very attached to us as a family. It would sit on Nigel's shoulder and snuggle into him. It was rarely in its cage and even though it flew out of the window one day, it must have decided it didn't like the outside world because it returned after a few hours. When we were leaving we thought about putting it in the aviary that was housed in the barracks but we didn't have the heart and so, at great expense, we brought it home.

We looked around the Taunton area for a new home and finally settled on a house called Pineda, near Chard. By this time Nigel had taken his O-Levels and was starting his A-Levels, and Gordon was living in London with friends. Gordon was very interested in music, particularly playing the guitar, and he was involved in that scene in London. It wasn't a world Ron and I understood really but he seemed happy enough. He kept in touch with Lynn, the American girl he'd met while at Dean Close School, and eventually she decided to move to London to be with him. Subsequently she would marry him at a very lovely ceremony in Combe St Nicholas, a village a couple of miles away from Chard, and it was the first time we'd met her American family.

Now, for the next part of the story we have to time-travel back to my early childhood, and the point at which my mother died and the family fell apart. You'll recall that I'd given some consideration to finding my sister June (whose twin sister Edith had, of course, died in the terrible car crash in Durham) but hadn't wanted to upset anyone. Well, by the late 1970s many years had passed since the twins were separated and Edith had been killed, and I thought now might be the time to revisit my original idea of placing an advert in the Newcastle Evening Chronicle to see if it may yield some clues. And in the next chapter, I will tell you what happened!

CHAPTER 15 – A LETTER FROM THE PAST

As you know, Aunt Eadie forbade me from referring to 'cousin' Edith as my sister and I've always regretted complying with this order, especially when Edith died so suddenly. The year 1978 would mark my 50th birthday and I was beyond caring about what people thought – including Aunt Eadie, who was still alive.

So one day in February 1978 I simply sat down and wrote a short letter to the editor of the Newcastle Evening Chronicle, explaining that I had a long-lost sister called June whom I was trying to find. I mentioned the Croftons, imagining that someone might remember them as they were a prominent family, and a bit about the circumstances of June's adoption.

I sent the letter and waited. For a few days I heard nothing. I rang the newspaper, to be told that the letter hadn't yet been published but it most certainly would be when a suitable slot was found. I was down in Somerset and therefore I couldn't see each evening's paper (this was long before the internet!) so I just had to trust the Letters Editor and hope for the best.

Shortly after this I'd been out one Saturday afternoon and

when I returned, Nigel (who was by then working towards his A-Levels) told me that I'd received a phone call. "An Eleanor somebody," he said, and that whoever it was had left a number.

So I rang it, and when a woman's voice answered I said that I was Mrs Olive Roberts, and that I'd been called by someone at this number.

"Oh," said the voice, "then you must be my sister."

The search was over, and I could barely believe I was speaking to someone I thought I'd never find again. "June?" I said, "is that really you?"

"No, it's not June," she said. "My name is Eleanor June, but I'm definitely your sister."

So, they'd kept part of her Christian name. I was desperate to hear more details about her, and although she'd rung me from work the minute she'd found out about the letter in the paper, we chatted for what seemed like ages as she told me more about herself. She had been adopted by a Jewish couple, the husband of which was a hairdresser. She hadn't been brought up Jewish, as she'd been christened, but she had been given another, more Jewish first name. She had no idea she had a sister (or stepsisters) and when she read my letter had had the shock of her life. After she and I had chatted, Ron took the receiver and also spoke with Eleanor June.

Then a day or so after this I received a letter. It was from Joyce Crofton (now Joyce Haile), the daughter of Charlie Crofton by his first marriage and the girl I got to know when I briefly lived with the family before my mother's sudden death. I hadn't seen or heard anything of her for more than 40 years so her letter was truly out of the blue. This is what it said:

> *"Dear Olive, it was a surprise reading your letter in the Chronicle last night.*
> *"Unfortunately I don't think I am able to help you in your*

search. All I know is that the other twin called June was adopted by a couple in the Gateshead/Low Fell area, and that the man was a barber/hairdresser.

"My father was most reticent about the adoption in his later years. When I enquired, he would only say that the baby had gone to a comfortable home, and that he had promised at the time never to get in contact with the child or to give any details. This he stuck to, and so no one in our family has ever known the name of the adoptive parents.

"I'm sorry I can't be of help. I only hope that someone else reading your letter – perhaps the girl (or now woman) – will get in touch with you. Yours sincerely, Joyce Haile (nee Crofton)."

Well, it was an unexpected surprise to get a letter from Joyce. It has to be remembered that she lost two stepsisters too, so I wrote back with thanks, and with a hope that one day we might meet up after such a long period being apart.

A day or so later I got another letter – another relative. This time it was Aunt Nancy, who had been alerted to my letter through her sister, Jessie. Again, we hadn't had contact for many years and after filling me in on some family news, she had this to say:

"I know you will want to know if I know anything, re your letter in the paper. Well Olive, I really don't know much, probably no more than you know yourself, as we were not told anything.

"I was at Earl's Drive when your mam died and I know the twins were taken to a nursery in West Parade in Benwell, but it is not there now, lots of (this area) has been demolished and Benwell has changed quite a lot.

"My Aunt once told someone that the other twin was adopted by a butcher and his wife in Gateshead but I'm afraid, Olive,

that is all I know, sorry, but you know I would help if I could.

"Have you heard from Joyce? I heard she was going to write to you, but my phone being out of order makes it awkward to get news.

"I would love you to let me know if you hear anything. I do hope you have some success, as it would be nice to find your twin stepsister.

"It was tragic about the other girls. I did see her once when I visited your Aunt in Durham, and I thought she was the image of Joyce.

"Is your Aunt still alive? I know she lost her husband. I used to write to her but you know how it is, one gets lazy at letter writing and then you lose touch.

"There are only three of us left out of a family of eight; myself, my sister Jessie and brother Mitchel. I wonder if you remember them.

"We always thought it was sad to have separated the twins, as I know the Aunt at Boldon wanted one, but of course it had nothing to do with us. Joyce has a very good husband and two very nice sons and a lovely home. Alan (Joyce's brother) is in Ireland and has two girls and one boy, so you see how people get separated.

"Well Olive, give me love to your hubby and family and please write some time."

If nothing else, at least I was reconnecting with members of my family I hadn't seen for many years. When I left East Boldon it was to move away properly and carve out a life of my own, which I had very much done, having had my own family and so many adventures abroad. Even so, it was good to know that during all my time away from the North East I hadn't been completely forgotten.

Eleanor, of course, was the only one who knew her

circumstances in detail and after I'd spoken to her by phone she wrote me a long letter. I hope you'll forgive me for printing it below in full, as it's an interesting account of how one's life can take a very unexpected turn. Attached to the letter was a picture of her holidaying by Lake Garda, Italy, the previous summer:

"Dear Olive, I have waited until after the weekend to write this letter and would ask you to make allowances for the fact that it is typewritten and not handwritten. I just could not collect my thoughts at home over the weekend and am just beginning to get back down to earth this morning. In the confines of my office I feel that I may be able to marshall my thoughts enough to give you an outline of the sort of person you have for a sister.

"As you will see from the photograph I am dark-haired, bespectacled and pleasantly plump. My friends feel that the two photographs I am sending you most closely resemble me because I am usually eating. I have blue eyes, I'm 5'5" small, and weight approx. 12 stone. Modesty prevents me from telling you what a nice person I am.

"I have lived all these years in the Gateshead/Newcastle area, having gone to school in Gateshead. I was privately educated at a school in Low Fell, Gateshead, which didn't really do me much good and set the cause of Independent School Education back about fifty years – I think it was because of me that the Government banned them from their subsidies list! Nevertheless, I pressed on with my efforts to avoid being educated and my parents embarked on a two-pronged attack by sending me on a Secretarial Course during the week and a course of Comptometer Operating on a Saturday morning. The Secretarial Course I quite enjoyed – it was at Skerry's College, Newcastle, and I could go out to lunch every day. Saturday mornings were somewhat of a trial as Mathematics was never a strong subject and the calculating machine became more of an obstacle than an

advantage because not only did I have to have knowledge of the machine but I had to apply my limited knowledge of maths to it. After about 10 mornings I decided that I was not cut out to be a Comptometer Operator and I played truant for about the next 15 weeks until one day my mother thought it was about time she had some kind of report from the school. The rest of the story needs no telling but Dad (also a mathless wonder) was on my side and common sense won through.

"And so I became a fully-fledged Secretary and the world was to be my oyster – well, not quite the world; my first job was as an office junior in the Greenmarket, Newcastle. Thirty bob a week and all the fruit and veg I wanted. After those lofty heights I went on to be a Shorthand-Typist for an Electrical wholesalers where I worked for 15 years until 10 years ago I had rather a serious nervous breakdown (from overwork!). I was in hospital for about six months and decided that once I was fit I would not return to that particular job. I signed on with an Agency and worked part-time for a few weeks and then as luck would have it the University of Newcastle were advertising for various posts and although I did not get any of the advertised ones I was approached by the Registrar's Office who offered me the job of Secretary to the Deputy Registrar. I worked for him for about two years and then applied for a transfer to my present department (German and Scandinavian Studies) where I have now become Administrative Secretary dealing with all administration for this rather large department. It's a job I love and I wouldn't change it for the world.

"Coming to the University has changed my life completely. Apart from the friendships I have made which are terrific, I have also become involved in many aspects of social and clerical matters. I was nominated as a member of a newly formed Clerical Staff Association when it was formed many years ago and I held various positions in the Association from Chairman to Social

Secretary. From this Association sprung a new branch of NALGO, the Trade Union which is now accepted by this University as its negotiating body, and I have been associated with the Union ever since. I am at present Branch Treasurer and Vice-Chairman. Don't get the impression I am a militant Trade Unionist – just the contrary in fact – I'm a reluctant one but there was no other way to improve our conditions of service and salary without an official Trade Union and all its know-how. So I am kept quite busy with Trade Union activities – weekends at Conferences; meetings; Schools etc., and I thoroughly enjoy it.

"What are my likes and dislikes? I like people (most of them anyway!), travel, music (listening and not playing), art, drama, driving, television, to name but a few things. I dislike unnecessary noise, women's lib, and cannot offhand think of anything else.

"As you know, I was adopted by a couple in this area (Mr and Mrs S. Ableman) at what must have been about three months of age. My childhood was not the most perfect but I did have a very comfortable home and an adoring father. My mother left a lot to be desired but that is another story. At the age of 17 it became apparent that my parents were on the verge of a split and if anyone had anything to do with the eventual split I suppose it was me. I made the decision for my father by booking him into a local hotel and helping him move into it. Life for him had been grim throughout the years but he stuck it for my sake and I felt the least I could do for him was to get him away to somewhere we could both be happy. It was around this time that it became necessary for him to tell me I was adopted and I think this must have been the hardest moment of his life. I have a rather humorous outlook on life and could only think of congratulating him on his extremely good taste in babies which made us both laugh and I think broke the ice for him. He, apparently, had always promised Charles Crofton that he would not disclose my parenthood during Crofton's lifetime and when eventually

Crofton died Dad felt it unnecessary to open up wounds again and therefore until your letter I never knew that I had any family although I had my suspicions. Dad is a very sick man and I would not wish him any unnecessary concern, therefore my desire to know more about my background was going to have to wait until he died. Dad is very relieved that I know the true facts now and is looking forward to meeting you as much as I am. He remarried eventually and still lives in Gateshead – I'm sure you will love him as much as I do.

"I moved out of the flat I shared with Dad when he remarried and I now share a house (which we are buying jointly) with a friend I met over 24 years ago. She worked at the same Electrical Wholesalers when I joined the Company but she now works for Proctor and Gamble Ltd., as a (would you believe it) Comptometer Operator (some people have all the brains). We have a lot in common and usually are taken for sisters rather than friends. We live in a three-bedroom semi together with a stray cat. Rita (my friend – not the cat) is three months younger than me and she lost her mother when she was 13; her father when she was 19; and gained my family when she was 19 1/2. She then lived with Dad and I for years until Dad remarried and then we set up house together. The flat we were in was somewhat overcrowded with three women in it.

"Neither Rita nor I have ever got married but it is not for lack of opportunity. I was engaged at 21 but the prospect of married bliss did not appeal to me (particularly with John) so I gave him his ring back and had a good holiday on the savings we scraped together. So as you can see I am also rather fickle.

"How do I feel now I know all the facts? Elated. I have always wanted brothers and sisters, nieces and nephews etc. I woke up on Saturday morning and was afraid it had all been some kind of dream and it wasn't until I went into the dining room and saw all my rather hastily written notes of addresses and

telephone numbers that I could believe that it had in fact happened. Not only do I have a sister who sounds terrific but I have a brother-in-law with a dark brown voice. It's difficult to put into words exactly how I feel. At first I was confused, then I was walking on air, and now I'm having to control my impatience to meet you all. Somerset seems a long way away at this present moment – I will be in London at a meeting in March but that seems too distant. I will be in Paris at the beginning of March so the weekend of March 3 is not possible. It really is unbearable not to be able to see you but I suppose I must contain myself.

Then, in her own handwriting, she added this:

"I have read through this rubbish and it strikes me that you will wonder how I ever became a Secretary in this University. My only excuse is that I am still not used to the idea of having a family and my more literary efforts will have to wait. I have decided to let you have a sample of my handwriting which you can see is no better than my typing.

"I am closing this letter now and hope it hasn't put you off me already. It all seems rather flippant but it is my way of coping with unusual situations. I hope we will meet soon. Love to everyone, from Eleanor."

Finally, I received a letter from someone unknown to me, a Sylvia Nicholson of Rowlands Gill, Tyne and Wear. She said:

"Dear Mrs Roberts, perhaps you will be kind enough to forgive me for writing to you, a total stranger, but I feel I must express the delight which at last your long search for your half-sister must have brought, certainly to Enid (she is known to her friends as Eleanor or Enid).

"She rang me up to tell me your news and she really is so

222

delighted but perhaps also a little sad that her twin sister had such a tragic death, only you will know if they are alike.

"My husband, myself and our son have known Enid and Rita (her friend whom you will now know she lives with) for the past 10 years - they became our neighbours and we have always been very good friends even after we both moved, even though we are still within eight miles of one another. Enid really is a most kind, generous and very considerate person and I am sure you will find great joy in each other. I know she is very much looking forward to meeting you; incidentally we have a small newsagent's shop in this village and I remember vaguely reading your letter and thinking, "I hope she has some luck" but never of course realised that I would know anyone concerned!

"We also know her adopted father and stepmother though have not seen them for some considerable time due to his ill health — they are also a charming couple and would always put themselves out to help people.

"Perhaps we will have the pleasure of meeting you in the none too distant future if you come North to visit Enid, which I'm sure you will."

Having set the wheels in motion, what did I make of all this? To me, Eleanor sounded an intelligent person but maybe not someone who'd had the easiest life. She seemed to have done well in her career and I was struck by the secretarial similarities between us. However, she appeared to have struggled with her mother and was somewhat insecure. It was easy to tell (by reading between the lines) that she was gay, which became clear when I went up to Newcastle to meet her and Rita.

All in all, we got on well and I liked her. In looks there was a familiarity too. Edith had resembled the Crofton side of the family far more than Eleanor, who looked like my mother and me. Thinking that she would pull out all the stops because she was her deceased daughter's twin, I took Eleanor to see Aunt Eadie. But she didn't pull out any stops whatsoever; in fact, she seemed rather annoyed that I'd brought her in the first place. So that was a bit of a disaster, only salvaged by the fact that she met Joyce Crofton and got on really well with her.

In August 1978 Eleanor and Rita came to visit us in Chard. We all had a good time and after they left I thought that here was someone with whom I could enjoy a good familial relationship, albeit one that had started later in life. While on holiday in Rhodes in the October of that year, Eleanor wrote Ron and I a letter thanking us for our hospitality:

> *"We really enjoyed our stay with you in August – we have told everyone about your beautiful home so you might get passers-by peering in at you during next summer. Have you got the garden finished? We are looking forward to sitting on the lawns next time we visit you – if you'll have us again. How is Sybil? When is my great niece/nephew due? I would knit something for it but no newly-born deserves that really. I didn't get past casting on and casting off at school without dropping stitches. Seriously though, do keep me informed. I haven't got used to being a sister yet but this is the first of my new family who will know me right from the start.*
>
> *"I want to say something now which may seem strange, but I do feel I have known both of you all of my life really. I'm comfortable with you and I know you are prepared to accept me as I am. I had a way of life before we met; they are my family, my friends, my work, and my existence. To them I owe what I am and what I have, and it would be wrong to drop them. I am trying to strike a happy medium but it is taking some time to adjust my commitments, to take in the family I have found. Obviously you, Ron and your family are my first choice but Joyce and Jack must get some thought as soon as I can when I get*

home. I met Jack on the train when I came down to Gatwick. He is very nice indeed and I would hate to upset them by my unintentional lack of interest. The truth is a lack of time which, when I try to explain it, seems a very poor and weak excuse. My time was pretty hectic before the news of a family – I hardly ever got to see Dad twice a month, never mind anything else. I feel guilty that I haven't had a chance to see the folks at East Boldon or go out to Durham. I'm full of good intentions, make my plans, and then something which is essential turns up and I'm lumbered once more. I suppose I'm asking you to act as my Father Confessor and forgive me my forgetfulness or whatever you may call it! Anyway you are very much in my thoughts and whilst thoughts are not everything, I do try to do what I can. So endeth the first sermon.

"It's getting rather late now so I will close for the time being. If you have a moment perhaps you could write or telephone. The telephone is usually my saviour I must admit. The problem is, as I have already said, I'm rarely in but Rita will be only too happy to give you all the news!

"Will you be coming North in the not-too-distant future? You are very welcome to stay with us any time you want. Just let us know. Love, Eleanor and Rita."

I couldn't quite put my finger on it but I felt there was something a little strange about Eleanor. At the time I put it down to a combination of a difficult childhood and a sense of shock at having gained a family. After more correspondence and visits, she finally wrote a letter to us asking if it would be possible to lend her £200. We were both a bit taken aback as this wasn't a small amount of money (in the late 1970s) and we were due to go out to America on holiday. Ron pointed this out, but also said that we wouldn't want to think she was going short, so he wrote back and agreed to lend her the money as long as she paid it back by

Christmas.

This was agreed, and Ron asked me to call her to make sure it was enough, and that she was alright and not in any trouble. So I did, but when I got through to a colleague in her office I was told that she'd flown off to Ibiza that very morning. We found this odd behaviour from someone who seemed to be needing money desperately, but we tried not to judge and when she came back Ron gave her a call. "If you really need that money you can keep it," he said, "and we don't want you to go short, but we are going to America and we could really do with it."

Well, she was a bit affronted by this and she said, "I have plenty of money and I can send you my bank account details to prove it." Ron replied that there was no need to do this, but she did it anyway and it was true – she certainly wasn't short of money. So why she needed some from us remained a mystery and she did pay it back in the end.

What became evident after a short while was that she was an alcoholic and very sadly she died from this illness some time during the mid-1980s. She'd had a difficult childhood and perhaps she also had some trouble with her sexuality. Back then, people knew about men being gay but perhaps it was harder for women to come to terms with it. I just don't know. But it was a sad end to her life, which hadn't really been the happiest, and a bittersweet conclusion to my story of finding her. Her death wasn't as sudden or shocking as that of the twin sister she never knew, but it was no less tragic for that.

CHAPTER 16 – ISLAND IN THE SUN

We enjoyed living in Chard but we were still up for adventures and when Ron got word that his next post would be Cyprus we began to pack our things with our usual mixture of anticipation and excitement.

We were just about at the end of the 1970s and Cyprus was still a tense place following the events of 1974, when the Turkish army invaded the north part of the island in response to the Greeks installing an anti-Turkish Cypriot candidate as president. Although the two sides had stopped fighting by the time we arrived there was a 'hard border' in place and a big British military presence on the island. We would be based in the British Army compound at Dhekelia – the first time we'd lived 'in barracks', so to speak – and we were given a month's notice to pack our things and get ready to go abroad.

We decided to let Gordon and his wife Lynn move into the house in Chard. It was a nice place and we wanted to keep it for when we returned. Nigel was by now at university in Manchester and needed a base for his holiday periods. So with all that in mind, and because we would be living in furnished accommodation in

Cyprus, we decided we'd take a more unconventional route to the island than to simply fly there.

It was Ron's suggestion that we drove there. "It'll be an experience, Olive," he said, and to that end we decided to buy a mobile home and drive across Europe to the Mediterranean. The boys were a bit shocked, and I think they hoped we'd abandon such rash plans. But we went ahead and purchased an old Transit van that had been converted into a caravanette. It was small but comfortable, and with the rest of our possessions travelling to Cyprus by sea, we simply packed what we needed and headed for Plymouth and the ferry to France. We'd already made sure that GCHQ were happy that we were travelling this way, and they agreed. So off we went.

Once in France, we did what every British tourist seemed to do at that time and headed for the nearest hypermarket to stock up on wine. These were the days when varieties of wine were very limited in British shops and so we marvelled at the rows upon rows of bottles, not having a clue about the contents of any of them.

These were still the winter months so we didn't do much sightseeing. Still, it was fun to stop in a different place every night and we slowly made our way through France to Italy, with the idea that we'd stay in Venice for a while before loading the Transit on to a ferry and heading to Greece. From there we'd explore Athens before getting another ferry across the Med to Cyprus.

Our arrival in Venice was met with some extremely cold and wet weather. Venice is a watery place anyway, so constant downpours made the whole city feel very dark and dank. It was quite deserted, and the only people around seemed to be wrapped up in their warmest winter clothes. We stopped for a couple of nights in a caravan park but it was rather a miserable experience so Ron suggested that we load the Transit on to the ferry and then spend the final night of our time in Venice in a hotel, which we knew would cheer us up.

So that's what we did, and being warm and dry made a pleasant change. The following day we walked down to the docks where the ferry was berthed to find there was a seamen's strike. No one seemed to be quite sure when we'd be leaving but we were told we could claim our berth aboard the ship and go into Venice for our food until the time came to set sail.

After a day or so we finally left Venice and we started to think about the places we'd like to see in Greece. One afternoon, as I was up on deck getting some fresh air, I was approached by a foreign man who engaged me in conversation. Ron was resting in the cabin and so I was alone. This man was tall, and in his late 50s or early 60s. He was charming and friendly, and soon we got talking like we were old friends. The man said he was Turkish, and when he asked me where I was going he seemed most interested in the fact that we were heading for Cyprus, where we'd be living on a British Army base on account of Ron's job.

Then Ron turned up. He sat down by us and listened to the conversation for a few minutes without saying much. When the man offered to buy him a drink, he refused. Then Ron turned to me.

"Olive," he said, "I think you and I need to go back to the cabin. There's something we need to discuss." And without further ado Ron took me by the arm and led me downstairs. On the way he asked a lot of questions about this man.

"He said he was Turkish," I said. "He was asking where we were off to and I told him Cyprus."

Ron groaned. "What else did you tell him?" he asked.

"Oh, just about the army and where we'd be staying and our time in Hong Kong and all that," I replied innocently.

"Do you know, Olive," Ron said, "during the first ever briefing I had with GCHQ I was told never to accept a drink from a stranger who wants to get you into conversation."

Then the penny dropped. The man was Turkish and he seemed very interested in the British Army in Cyprus. I felt a fool for not spotting it earlier. Perhaps he was just being friendly but now I began to have my doubts. Plus, he was wearing perfume – maybe that should have rung alarm bells from the beginning.

Anyway, we had no further contact from this passenger and when we arrived in Greece we drove over to Athens as planned and looked at all the marvellous sights connected with ancient Greece, including the Acropolis of course.

After our time there we boarded another ferry and headed for the port of Limassol, in Cyprus. There, we drove the caravanette off the ship and straight into the customs area. Well, to say the Greek Cypriots took the thing apart is an understatement. Never mind that we were part of the British garrison on the island; they seemed to want to know everything about us. They even asked us if we were smuggling a dog in the Transit because they spotted a leather strap dangling down from the roof that raised the lid, and assumed it was a dog's collar! Then they got into a real state about the wine we still had stashed away from our travels through France. They completely refused us to take even a drop into Cyprus and to our shock they opened every bottle and emptied them by the roadside.

Then the customs men started on the potatoes... believe it or not, they even objected to the fact that we had a few leftover spuds in the van. I suppose they believed that Cyprus potatoes were the best in the world and that any imports were an insult! Anyway, they took it seriously enough to drop the potatoes by the side of the van then stamp on them. We were astonished, but after this they let us through and we started out for Dhekelia.

As we drove up from Limassol I saw how barren and dry Cyprus was. The roads were dusty and lined with rubbish, and a smell of gasoline hung in the air. Dhekelia itself was up near the UN 'buffer zone' keeping apart the Greek Cypriots and Turkish

Cypriots, who were still very much hostile to one another. The vibrancy and love of life we'd experienced in Singapore and Hong Kong seemed to be entirely absent from this place; in fact the atmosphere was one of tension and depression. I really wondered what we'd let ourselves in for and my opinion didn't change when we arrived at the camp and saw our living quarters. The 'apartment' that sounded quite glamorous back in the UK was very basic indeed and there was very little we could do with it to make it more comfortable. Even after our furniture arrived we couldn't escape the barracks-atmosphere of the place. It didn't help matters that our quarters were normally of the sort reserved for sergeants and Warrant Officers; without wanting to sound snobbish there were friends of ours who were allocated officer-standard accommodation and by comparison it seemed as though they'd been elevated to the peerage!

Anyway, being the sort of people we are we determined to make the best of it. I had no children with me and I wasn't working, so really the world should've been my oyster. And perhaps that was the problem, because there was very little to do when your husband was out working all day. The local towns were nothing to write home about and you weren't able to visit the greener and apparently more interesting side of the island because the Turks were occupying it. We had friends of course, but I didn't want to spend all day moaning to them about how bad Cyprus was. I would've turned into the kind of person who first picked us up in Singapore all those years ago. So while Ron was working I looked round for something to amuse me.

Ron brought his passion – cameras and photography – with him to Cyprus and as he usually did in new places, he started a camera club. He was particularly good on the technical side and would give patient instruction to new members who had very little experience. One afternoon he'd taken out a group of people to show them how to 'pan' – a trick which involved pressing the shutter while following something moving (a vehicle for example), resulting in an interesting, blurred image.

The following day two English men in plain clothes knocked on the door and asked for Ron. He was out at work, and I told them this.

"What time is he back?" one of them asked.

"In about an hour," I said. "But I never know quite how long he'll be out."

"Then we'll wait," the other man said, and the two of them trooped off to sit in their car and keep an eye on our apartment. This made me uneasy, and when Ron arrived home I immediately pointed out the two men. By then, they were already out of the car and walking back up the path.

"What's this about, then?" Ron asked as the men approached. In response, one produced an ID card and showed it to Ron.

"We're from MI5," one of them said. "Can I ask you why you and others were taking pictures of cars on the road outside the base yesterday?"

Ron explained that he was part of a camera club and had been innocently giving fellow members a lesson in panning. "We know where you work," one of the men replied, "and we're concerned about your activities."

Then the men explained that one of the cars Ron and students had been photographing had been occupied by a couple of MI5 agents. Ron wasn't to know this, of course, and he'd certainly not done anything deliberately, but the agents were worried enough to demand that Ron take them to the camera club HQ and give up all the film that he and the other members had taken. They also went through our house from top to bottom, looking for any prints he may have made.

Ron's reaction was typically laconic. "Oh, these bloody people making a fuss about nothing," he commented. I was worried he might be arrested for spying or something but he was more het up about the fact they hadn't believed him immediately and that he'd had to get the Base Commander to vouch for him.

I can't say I really liked Cyprus as a place to live, not in the way I'd enjoyed Singapore and Hong Kong. I didn't mind the constant heat, which was regularly tempered by a cool breeze blowing up from the coast. It was a lack of very much to do that bothered me. It really was quite boring. The Cypriot towns weren't much to write home about and there was a tension right across the island that you could almost taste. Having done all the work I did in Hong Kong I was used to military life, and although we had the Chinese across the border there was little to no tension felt on the island. Cyprus was different. The war between the Greeks and the Turks had been brutal, bloody and recent. There was no compromise on either side and you felt anything could happen at any moment.

That said, we were intrigued about the north side of the island, the part that was under Turkish occupation. It was said to be the most beautiful part of Cyprus, despite the fighting. There was a limited amount of access to North Cyprus via the various checkpoints, but given the nature of Ron's job it wasn't advised that we should make the crossing.

We used to go down to the coast at Ayia Napa in our mobile home. There was a lovely little beach there, populated by Brits, and of course we got talking to people as we enjoyed the Cypriot sunshine. We became quite friendly with a group of people who worked at the British High Commission, and during one conversation we were asked if we'd travelled over to the 'other side'.

"No," we said, "but it sounds very interesting."

"Well," said one of the men Ron was chatting to, "would you like to come with us?"

As you're probably aware by now, Ron and I were always up for an adventure, and although we knew we shouldn't, we decided to take our new friends up on their offer. It was for a day only, so we were picked up by jeep and taken over the border at the famous 'Black Knight' crossing point at Azios Nikolaos.

The first place we visited was the ruined 13th century Bellapais Abbey, which would've been beautiful had the Turkish army not been taking pot-shots at the pigeons roosting in there. There was blood all over the walls and feathers everywhere, which was upsetting.

Then we stopped off at the port of Kyrenia and had a drink by the semi-circular harbour. That really was an impressive place, and despite the damage caused by the war I could see why people said the north was the better side of the island. Even so, it was sad to see vandalised and neglected Greek Orthodox churches everywhere. I must say that the Greeks did a much better job of looking after abandoned mosques on 'their' side of the island.

Finally we went to the Karpaz, the 'pan-handle' of Cyprus and again, the landscape was impressive even if a fair few of the buildings were in a poor state. We came back via Nicosia, pleased to have seen a 'secret' part of Cyprus and not been found out!

I'd decided I wouldn't work on this tour. Perhaps that was a mistake because it left me with nothing to do when Ron was at work. I realised I couldn't go on like this indefinitely and so I made a determined effort to get to know the other wives, military and civilian, who were also out there kicking their heels. One day I was chatting to a group of women in a coffee shop and I was asked if I'd ever played golf. Well, I hadn't but I was willing to give anything a go. So this lady said, "If you can get your hands on a couple of golf clubs, I'll show you the basics."

A few days later I'd cobbled together an old set of clubs and I made my way to the local golf club. I hadn't a clue about golfing technique, rules or etiquette but this lady was very patient and after a couple of hours on the practice ground I found I was quite enjoying myself, even if I was just trying to see how far I could hit the ball! At the end of the session I decided I'd enjoyed myself enough to go back - and I did, very regularly. One day, as I was practising my swing (I knew all the terminology by now) a lady from the club approached me.

"We've noticed you've been coming here regularly," she said, indicating a group of women just about to tee off on the first hole. "Why don't you join us? We're thinking about setting up a dedicated ladies' club. No men! How about it?"

So we went for a coffee and a chat, and that's how I got into golfing. The ladies recommended which clubs to use and gave me a good grounding in the rules. So that was one way I kept the boredom at bay. The other way was through painting. I hadn't drawn or painted since I was at school and I seemed to remember getting my knuckles rapped for drawing a ladder the wrong way around against a tree or something. In any case, I hadn't followed up any interest I might have had in art post-school and it was only when I was passing the education centre on the base at Dhekelia and saw a notice about a new watercolours class that I decided to give it a go.

And, like the golf, I seemed to take to it quite naturally. I discovered I had a good eye for colour and line, and the lady running the group noticed this too. She complimented me on the work I was doing while telling me that her husband was the base's Commanding Officer. I asked who he was, and when she said he was an Irish colonel it was my chance to tell her that I'd worked for a few high-ranking officers in Hong Kong. She asked me who they were and when I mentioned that one of them was Brigadier Sibbald her eyes lit up.

"What a coincidence!" she said. "He's a General now and he's coming out to visit us next week. You absolutely must meet him again, Olive."

So we did meet up and he seemed very pleased to see me again. We had a nice chat, and I think he'd forgiven me for being poached from his office by Bunny Burnett. It was good to meet someone who could reminisce so fondly about Hong Kong and it just made me miss the place even more.

Eventually the art group left the classroom and we started to visit local landmarks, painting them then having lunch. We'd hold regular exhibitions at which everyone bought everyone else's work. When Ron had free weekends or days we'd go to the beach or up into the Troodos Mountains. It was said that in Cyprus you could be swimming in the morning and skiing in the afternoon and it was true, though I never actually learned to ski. I did do a bit of sledging, however!

Otherwise, we'd try to keep ourselves entertained by visiting local restaurants or taking in occasional Greek festivals where there might be a bit of song, dance and wine. But generally I was quite bored and I would regularly catch scheduled RAF flights back to England. These were offered via Forces Network Radio, which I listened to regularly, and were cheap, no-frills affairs aboard old VC-10s but I didn't care. Within five hours I'd be touching down at Brize Norton and delighted to be home again. Sometimes I'd just jump on a plane with very little advance warning and once home I'd ring Colin, hoping he wouldn't mind picking me up at short notice.

After three years Ron's tour was up and needless to say I was very pleased to be returning permanently. We still had the house in Chard that Gordon and Lynn had been living in, and by this stage they'd decided to up sticks and go to live in the United States. So after yet another adventure we were back in Somerset, and more than glad to be home.

CHAPTER 17 – ACTIVE RETIREMENT

While we'd been away in Cyprus there had been a big change in UK politics. Margaret Thatcher was now Prime Minister and her time in office would in many ways come to define the decade. As a family we were split on our opinion of her, as I imagine many British families were. Nigel was Conservative and loved her; Colin was Labour and did not. Gordon was now in America and supporting the Democrats so I expect he had little time for her either. I was neutral, understanding that things had to change but realising that when they did there could be a great deal of damage caused as a result.

Ron was not a Thatcher supporter. He was always a Labour man and a Trade Unionist, and he was very proud of this, but by the time he returned to work in Taunton the union he'd helped to set up at GCHQ was under severe threat from the Conservative government. In 1981 there had been a series of strikes by GCHQ staff in response to a dispute over pay. At the time GCHQ wasn't a publicly acknowledged organisation; although many people in Cheltenham and other parts of the country were connected to it, it remained something of a secret.

But it seemed that the pay dispute and the strike had rattled the Americans, who had significant interests in the work of GCHQ, and apparently it was their influence that led Mrs Thatcher to consider a ban on trade union activity within the organisation on the grounds of national security.

Well, there was outrage when this became knowledge within GCHQ circles. Ron was particularly incensed because he'd worked so hard to establish union rights in the workplace and he felt this was now being taken from him and every other union member with little to no consultation. This was made even more fractious by the Government offering every union member £1,000 to leave the union and instead join a 'staff association', or be dismissed. Ron was a man of principle and would never have been 'bought' by such an arrangement. Besides, he was approaching his 60th birthday and so he began to consider his options for possible retirement.

There were other factors at work too. Ron had joined the fledgling GCHQ just after the Second World War, when the primary way of communicating secretly was by Morse Code. By now, in the early 1980s, the organisation was computerised and while Ron did keep up with developments it wasn't always easy. He spilled tea into the first computer he ever worked on, which didn't end well, and he felt that computers took away the personal element of the work he did, which to him made a great deal of difference.

Increasingly he would return home after a shift grumbling about changes at work or the new technology that was making him frustrated and giving him metaphorical headaches. He considered a new career teaching photography but then realised that if he left and got another job he would lose much of his pension rights. So he decided to apply for early retirement instead.

In the meantime we picked up the threads of our life in Chard, connecting with our old friends and the hobbies we had before we went to Cyprus. Ron continued his photography and the running of various camera clubs, while I improved on my painting and golf and also delivered 'meals on wheels' for the Women's Royal Voluntary Service. We had a host of friends and relatives come to visit now we were back in England, including Clem Foster, an Australian serviceman who worked in signals when we were out in Singapore, and with whom we both got on very well. He contacted us to say that he had been posted to a course at GCHQ and that he'd very much like to visit us while he was in England.

However, the only weekend he had available coincided with the FA Cup Final. Ron and Nigel (who was back from university then) were avid football fans and not even a visitor from 12,000 miles away was going to put them off a Saturday afternoon in front of the TV. "No worries," said Clem cheerfully, "football's not my thing anyway. Bit of a Pommie game, if I'm honest."

Then Clem asked Ron if it was alright for him to take me out for a drive. So while Ron and Nigel discussed teams and tactics Glen escorted me to his hire car and we set off for a day in Devon. We headed in the direction of Torquay and the English Riviera, and had the most wonderful time. Clem was particularly taken by the rows of beach huts by the sea and couldn't believe that people got changed and had refreshments in them. "Ain't that a Pommie thing?" he remarked as he took dozens of photographs. We arrived back quite late at night, to the relief of Ron and Nigel who seemed surprised that we'd not made it back in time for the Cup Final. In fact, they were so worried they called the police and local hospitals to see if we'd been in an accident! I'm still in touch with Clem, and recently I saw on Facebook that he'd posted a picture of a cream tea he was about to have. "That's a bit of a Pommie thing," I remarked cheekily.

As I mentioned, Gordon and Lynn vacated the house and moved to Maryland on our return to Britain. Their moving-out wasn't in the best of circumstances and we didn't hear from them for quite a while afterwards. Then one day a letter arrived bearing an unfamiliar stamp and postmark. The letter was from Gordon and it was a nice, chatty account of how they'd settled into life in the United States, finding a house and jobs, and that they would like us to visit some time. We were pleased, and began to make plans to see a country we'd never experienced before.

Ron's situation at work was becoming more and more difficult, what with the anti-union legislation about to be passed and all the protests around it. Plus, a younger crowd were moving into GCHQ; university-educated but without the military experience that Ron and his associates had had from the Second World War. Ron simply wasn't happy anymore, and was relieved when in the later part of 1983 his application for early retirement was granted, with effect from December 31.

Ron had had 36 years' service with the GPO and GCHQ. With his wartime service in the RAF and the Royal Navy, this came to a total of 40 years. No one could ever say that he hadn't done his 'bit' for the country, and on New Year's Eve 1983 he drove out of the gate at his base in Taunton for the last time. On that occasion I was waiting for him at the gate and I remember him taking off his pass and handing it in to the guard with a bewildered look. It was the end of an era.

"Well," he said, as I got into the passenger seat, "that's it, Olive. I haven't got my pass anymore and it feels very strange. What will I do now?"

"You can do anything you want," I said, taking his hand in mine. "You're a free man, so don't worry about it."

"I'm not worried, Olive," he said laughing. And so we set off home to enjoy what would be almost 25 years of retirement, though Ron never referred to it as that. He always said he was 'on the pension' and was delighted by the increasing number of years he spent on it. We were lucky in that sense, because many couples don't enjoy even half that time together.

Soon after retirement we took up Gordon's offer of a visit to America and were knocked out by what we experienced. It was to be the first of many trips across the Atlantic and we were always made to feel very welcome by our family and their friends.

Gordon and Lynn were working hard, and long hours too, so quite often they'd only get in late. But we had the use of a car and so we travelled around Maryland and into Virginia, North Carolina and Kentucky. We went to see various battlefields dating from the Civil War and we were amazed by the beautiful Blue Ridge Mountains. We also went to Kansas City by Greyhound bus with the intention of stopping for a few days on arrival. This was quite a journey because the bus stopped at every little place en route. However, our fellow passengers were incredibly friendly and soon we were chatting as though we'd known everyone for years. People even offered to swap seats with us so we could have a better view of the scenery passing by. I can't imagine that ever happening in Britain. By the time we arrived in Kansas City it was quite dark and we hadn't a clue how to get to our hotel from the bus station. The bus driver asked us if we knew the way and when we said 'No' he picked up the microphone from the tannoy and switched it on.

"OK everyone," he said. "Now I hope all y'all don't mind, but Olive and Ron from England here don't know the way to their hotel, so I'm gonna take them to the door. If that's all right with y'all."

In response, everyone cheered and soon we were right outside our hotel, the bus driver helpfully unloading our bags from the luggage compartment. How's that for service?

We liked America and Americans and as I've said, we went back several times. We did have the occasional strange moment, for example in a town close to where Gordon and Lynn were living. Gun law seemed to be the rule there and we could hear the odd shot ringing out as we walked down the main street. We went for lunch in a café but had to vacate it quickly because someone was prowling around with a gun. Things like that I found hard to deal with, and also the attitude towards black people in some of the southern states. I really didn't like that atmosphere at all. Luckily my family had no such problems towards people of a different colour and they counted several black families among their friends.

During this period we moved to a detached house that was smaller than our current place, but much closer to town. It was pleasant to be able to take a short walk into Chard and we considered that since we were unlikely to be living abroad again, we'd found the place we'd settle in for the rest of our lives.

Now, you're probably wondering how many places we'd lived by now and to be quite honest I'm not really sure. At the time of writing this I think I've lived in 26 houses! I really do need to think back and have a proper count-up. Anyway, I know it's quite a number. As circumstances would have it, we wouldn't be too long in our new house before we were packing again and putting our home on the market. We weren't going abroad – in fact, we were heading 'home' to our roots - but I guess there would be those in Somerset who would consider the North East of England to be a long way abroad!

Our journey back up the country was prompted by news of Ron's sister, Edna, who at that time was very ill and needed looking after. We knew we couldn't keep driving up and down the country regularly and to be quite honest we were both quite intrigued by the idea of going home. We'd been away for so long that we now felt somewhat rootless and we thought it would be nice to re-connect with our shared origins.

During our visits to the North East we began to look at properties and naturally we realised that we could get quite a bit more for our money up there. I had a cousin in Hexham who helped us with the research and eventually we came across a new estate being built in Shotley Bridge, a village close to the town of Consett. There were a few houses already on the market there, so we got to know the builder and eventually we put a deposit down on a lovely long white bungalow with a frontage and half an acre of land at the back.

They say that if you've left a place you shouldn't go back for any length of time. Sadly in our case that turned out to be true. Initially it felt wonderful to be in familiar surroundings but we soon realised that the place we'd come 'home' to wasn't the place we'd left. And how could it have been? We'd last lived there more than 30 years before and while it was still a beautiful area full of friendly folk, the decline of its big industries and the effect this had on communities was painful to see. Besides, many if not most of the relatives we still had living in the North East seemed to be falling ill and we spent a huge amount of time commuting between various hospitals. This list of casualties included Ron, who had by this time developed cataracts. He'd already had one operated on in Taunton but now the other one was causing him difficulties. However, when we went to see the specialist in Newcastle we were told there was quite a waiting list and were advised that since he'd had the other one done in Taunton, we might be better off enquiring there. This is what we did and as it turned out there was far less of a wait, so Ron had the operation and I was tasked with driving back to the North East.

Now, I'd had a provisional driving licence for many years but never had proper lessons. Ron had taken me out when we lived in Kent but as in so many husband-tries-to-teach-wife-to-drive situations, this was a bit of a disaster. I remember driving the old Post Office van somewhere around Rye, with the kids in the back, and Ron being very tense. There was a puddle in the road, which I hit full on, spraying water all over the windscreen. Ron made me stop and wipe all the water away, then we continued along in stony silence. Then he made another remark so I stopped the car, got out and told him I would walk home.

"Get back in!" he shouted, "or I'll run you over!"

I'm sure he didn't mean that (!) but the whole experience was enough to put me off driving for years – until Ron began to have problems with his eyes and necessity meant that I'd have to take some lessons. These began when we were in Chard, at the insistence of Colin and Nigel, and although I was reluctant I knew I'd have to give driving a try. So I took some lessons, booked a test – and promptly failed it. I didn't get much further than the first roundabout. I went with another driving instructor, hoping for a better result, but again I failed.

Then I was told about a former police officer who'd become a driving instructor following his retirement. He had a great reputation for getting people like me through their tests, so I booked him and he was everything people had said about him; patient and understanding but very firm and on the ball. I can't say I enjoyed these lessons, or driving in general (I think the effect of my sister and cousin being killed so horrifically in the car crash had impacted on my mind forever), but anyway I got as far as a third test.

My instructor came with me on the day of the test, telling me I'd know if I'd passed because the examiner would ask me to produce my licence. When we arrived, the waiting room was full of people and there was a backlog because several examiners were off with the 'flu. I was assigned to the man in charge of the test centre, who hardly ever did any examining personally.

When we got into the car he turned to me and said, "Now just settle down and take me for a drive. We don't need to talk – just concentrate on the road and you'll be fine."

So I followed this basic instruction and tried to relax, although it wasn't easy with this man watching my every move. At one point I made a joke about driving around a slalom (perhaps I was on a roundabout) but he didn't laugh. Eventually he asked me to drive back to the test centre.

"Well, Mrs Roberts," he said, "I am going to pass you today. But what you need to do, and as soon as possible, is go out and learn to drive on your own."

I was delighted to have passed but understandably nervous about going it alone. However, Ron insisted and the following day I gingerly edged the car out of our driveway and in the direction of the local garden centre some 25 miles away. I made it there safely, then parked up and bought a few things from the shop. When I returned, however, I couldn't remember for the life of me how to reverse the car out of the parking space. Luckily, there was a man nearby who offered to help and after that I always made sure that wherever I parked there would be a ready supply of nice men willing to help me out – especially in multi-storey car parks which were the bane of my life.

Anyway, I carried on like this for a number of years and I suppose I got used to popping to the shops and visiting friends. Then I began to develop difficulties with my own eyes and I knew that my driving days were numbered. I wasn't so bad during the day but driving at night became more and more difficult, so rather than risk my own life (and those of other road users!) I decided to pack it in. After Ron died I gave my car, a Honda Jazz, to my daughter-in-law Sybil in Cheltenham but she didn't like driving either and eventually she brought it back. So I sold it and used the money to help finance a lovely family holiday to Hong Kong to celebrate my 80th birthday.

But now we're jumping forward into the future and we're not quite there yet. To go back to the story… we were in the North East for about three years and, as I've mentioned, we came back to the South West briefly so that Ron could have his other cataract operated on. We'd started to notice that, living in the North East, we were seeing less of our grandchildren than we'd like, just because of the distance involved in travelling and Ron's eyes not being up to long journeys. Soon after his sister died we reflected on our situation and agreed that while our roots would always be in the North East, our families, friends and all the people we knew and loved were down south. So once again we were on our travels.

CHAPTER 18 – FAME AT LAST

Our intention was to return to the Cheltenham area. Colin was close by and Nigel was in Cardiff, which isn't really so far away – certainly a lot closer than Consett. We started looking around Cheltenham and soon we realised that unlike the move from south to north, we would now get less for our money coming the opposite way.

We couldn't believe how prices had rocketed while we'd been away and we couldn't find anything we liked within our budget. We began to have doubts about Cheltenham and we didn't really want to move back to Bishops Cleeve (having learned our lesson about moving back anywhere) so we decided to broaden our search around the Gloucestershire area.

Coincidentally, at the same time we decided to have a holiday in the Forest of Dean and we really liked the area. When I was running the Guides group in Bishops Cleeve we'd camped in the Forest of Dean and always had a great time. An exploration of various estate agents' windows and a flick through the local paper confirmed that unlike Cheltenham, this area was very affordable for us. We came across a house for sale in Coleford that we thought would be suitable for us. It was a nice detached house that had plenty of room for us and our dogs. We had two King

Charles Cavaliers, Robbie and Kim, and they very much enjoyed all the walks around this interesting and hidden part of Gloucestershire.

The house was a new-build and before we moved in we noticed a number of dogs in the property next door. That didn't bother us – until we found out that our neighbours were dog breeders, and that their dogs barked day and night. That didn't bother us much either but many of the other neighbours were upset, particularly when the breeders would get their prize dogs ready for the annual Crufts show by letting them out at 3am. We did complain about this, to be told that the dogs needed exercise because they'd be cooped up all day.

Generally, though, we didn't mind much and it certainly didn't spoil our time living in this unique area of the country, although our neighbours close by were frustrated; so much so that one day, as I was out in the garden, I got a soaking from a hosepipe pointed over our fence. "Oi!" I shouted, "what have you done that for?"

"Just keep those bloody dogs quiet!" a man shouted back.

"But they're not my dogs that are barking!"

Anyway, I'm sure we would've stayed much longer there but by this time Nigel and Bella had had their first child, Catherine, and we spent a fair amount of time travelling across to Chippenham, where they were (followed by a later move to Malmesbury) to do our bit with the babysitting. Then Bella had the twins and it dawned on us that instead of all this travelling, we should just move closer to them, and to Colin too.

So we looked around Chippenham and found a place we both liked in Gascelyn Close. It was a semi-detached house on a small estate and we liked it because it had a nice big garden. Nigel and Bella were aware that the area wasn't the greatest in Chippenham but that didn't bother us really. Not long after we moved in it became clear that Nigel and Bella were right. The place seemed to be a haven for drug-taking, joy riding and all kinds of criminal goings-on.

And yet, we didn't mind all that too much. In fact, Ron thought it was fascinating. He watched at the living room window as people hid drugs in a nearby hedge before someone on a motorbike came to pick them up. "Come and have a look, Olive!" he'd shout, as yet another shady deal was happening outside. I'd come to the window and we'd laugh as whoever it was attempted to hide his drugs in the bushes. Nigel and Bella were horrified and worried for us, but we liked the area and the neighbours, plus I had a nice big garden. Despite everything, we were happy there.

Nigel and Bella, however, didn't share our enthusiasm for the area. They worried about us a lot, despite Ron getting to know a few of the local tearaways, who referred to him as 'granddad'. He'd spend a morning sweeping up fallen leaves on the pavements then watch as the local kids rode their bikes right through the middle of them. "Bloody kids," he'd say, quietly smiling.

One day I'd been out shopping with Bella in Malmesbury and we were driving home when she made a slight detour towards Milbourne Park – I suppose you'd describe it as the posher end of town, full of nice bungalows and well-kept gardens.

"A quick look around won't do any harm," said Bella, "and you never know, we might find something that grandpa likes."

'You'll be lucky,' I thought. Wherever we went, Ron seemed to have a habit of not wanting to move to anything he'd deem 'too fancy'. I usually managed to persuade him but it could be a battle. As we drove around Milbourne Park I could almost hear his reaction when I'd mention what Bella and I had been doing earlier in the day.

"Milbourne Park?!" he said, when I got him that night. "Oh no… not a chance, Olive. It's too expensive up there. Too expensive and too posh. I don't want to live in that place."

I told him we'd spotted a bungalow up there that needed a bit of attention, and that it was quite reasonably priced. Reluctantly he agreed to see it, but when we went up there, full of expectation, he turned it down immediately. "No," he said, "not on your nelly will I buy this place. Too much work needs doing."

Certainly, work did need doing, and not just on the house. If we were to get Ron to move we'd need a big family effort to help him change his mind. Eventually that worked and off we went up to Milbourne Park. The house was knocked to bits as we made a lovely open-plan space, complete with a conservatory at the back. I'm not sure Ron ever truly loved the place but he made the best of it and I liked it because it had a lovely garden - great for our two dogs, Robbie and Kim - and was on a bus route into town.

Life was good. We were close to Nigel and Colin, we lived in a nice neighbourhood and we enjoyed seeing our grandchildren regularly. Retirement held out a lot of possibilities for us. But like many other people our age, our bodies started to give up on us, little by little. Back in Taunton, Ron had been in and out of hospital with prostate trouble which led to chronic backache, so he suffered on and off from that. He always smoked (I gave up when I was in my 50s) and so there were always a few issues around his general health.

However, it wasn't Ron's problems but mine which landed us in hospital in Bath in the latter part of 2006. For a while I'd noticed that my vision wasn't as it should be – but only in the middle of my eye. My peripheral vision was fine, but it was as if someone had wiped some Vaseline in the centre of my eye, making my central vision cloudy. I knew who people were but I was finding it hard to see the expression on their faces. And yet, if I looked at them in the corner of my eye I could see them just fine.

Just before Christmas 2006 I was diagnosed with 'wet age-related macular degeneration' and was told that unless I had regular injections I would go blind. The problem was that these injections were not then available on the NHS in our area, which came under Wiltshire Primary Care Trust (PCT), and it was the same in almost all regions of England and Wales. The injections would cost more than £600 each – a large amount of money every month. This was because they hadn't yet been ratified by the National Institute for Clinical Excellence (NICE) for use by the NHS and could only be obtained privately.

Coincidentally, and ironically, at the same time Ron started to notice similar problems with his eyes. He too attended hospital in Bath and just a week after me he was diagnosed with the same condition. Now we had a real problem. We couldn't afford £600 each to fund this treatment and although we waited a while to see if the local PCT would somehow make an exception for us, it became clear quite quickly that our hopes would be dashed. In fact, despite contacting them with letters of support from our doctor we heard nothing back from them for ages, and we'd been told that time was of the essence. The quicker we could get the injections the better the results would be for our sight. We had no idea what we should do and as we went into 2007 we were forced to accept that because we could only afford one course of treatment, one of us would have to go blind. So who would that be?

In Ron's mind, there was no question. He was always a strong character, and a man committed to doing what he thought was the right thing. He wouldn't have dreamt of letting me suffer unnecessarily. "Of course it's going to be you who has the treatment, Olive," he said, "I'll soldier on, I'm sure."

Even so, as a family we felt that even having to make such a decision was wrong, and that there were many people out there being forced to go blind through no fault of their own. Many of them wouldn't be able to afford treatment for themselves, never mind for their husband or wife too. Nigel and Bella were incensed, arguing that we'd paid into the National Insurance scheme all our lives and that we were entitled to receive help. We agreed, and so began a campaign that quickly saw us all over the newspapers and on the TV and the radio – at the ages of 78 and 81, suddenly we were celebrities!

We contacted various organisations including the Royal National Institute of the Blind. They agreed that our case was extraordinary and told us they would take it up with the PCT as soon as possible. They were as good as their word and in early March 2007 we received the amazing news that, after a meeting, the PCT would make an exception and fund my treatment. That meant we could start my treatment straight away, though we were told Ron needed more tests before the PCT could decide the best treatment for him.

The RNIB were also very pleased, but they pointed out that funding for macular degeneration across the UK was a 'postcode lottery' and that things needed to change. They also said that 80 per cent of PCTs weren't funding such treatment and that 50 people per day risked losing their sight because they couldn't access treatments on the NHS. Obviously, there was a lot of campaigning work to be done and we were determined not to give up on Ron's case.

As he'd always been a man of principle Ron felt strongly that he was entitled to free treatment. He discovered that he was his own best spokesperson and many were the times I handed the phone to him so that he could talk to the media. He said this to the Western Daily Press:

"I've got my principles and I refuse to pay for this. My principles are more important than my eyesight, I suppose. Aneurin Bevan said that the NHS would help people from cradle to grave. Well, it has served me well from the cradle but now I'm approaching the grave it isn't doing too well anymore.

"I realise that the NHS hasn't got a bottomless pit of money but my pot of gold isn't all that big either. I have paid into the

NHS all my life and now I feel entitled to it. MY wife is very important to me so she is the one receiving the treatment but I think we should both have it free."

Ron's wartime service and subsequent career with GCHQ didn't do his case any harm either. The media focused in on his 'Blitz spirit' and Ron always told them he would never give up fighting for what he believed was right. In short, he became a local hero.

The treatments, which involved having liquid injected directly into the eye, weren't very pleasant but at least it meant my eyesight wouldn't get any worse. The people at the hospital decided they would get Ron in for assessment, which gave him hope that he would win the battle both for his eyesight and for NHS funding for him and everyone else with AMD.

I find it very hard talking about the next part of this story so I'm going to ask Bella, my daughter-in-law, to help. She and Nigel were very good about taking me to and from the Royal United Hospital (RUH) in Bath, where I had my injections, and they were determined that our hopes and fears should be heard by those in authority, even when those very people didn't want to listen to what we had to say.

Chapter 19 – Goodbye to Ron

Towards the end of March 2007 I was starting to have regular appointments at the RUH in Bath. As I've mentioned, Bella, Nigel and Colin were very good about taking me to and from the hospital because I could no longer drive due to my eyesight. Even if I could've driven I wouldn't have – I'd long lost my confidence on the roads and to be truthful I never had much of it for driving to start with.

The Health Authority people had already said they would assess Ron to see what could be done for his eyes, and we were hopeful that he'd be funded too, especially after all the fuss we'd made. We'd heard that the press coverage generated by our campaign had led to other Trusts and health authorities across the UK agreeing to fund injections for people with AMD, which delighted us immensely. Even if Ron couldn't get funding he could at least be pleased that he'd helped other people with the condition, and in the future too.

That said, I could see the stress the whole issue was having on him. As I've mentioned, he'd suffered on and off from various things for years but now everything seemed to be taking its toll.

We'd both been called into hospital to be tested on a new machine that took very detailed pictures of the eye. This had been purchased by the Friends of the Royal United Hospital and, following our campaign, they wanted us to be the first to use it. We received a date for this appointment and I'm right in thinking that we travelled together with Bella. Then Ron was called back for a further assessment and again, Bella took him. At this point, she will continue to tell the story:

> *"I didn't mind helping out with the driving to the RUH. Ron wouldn't normally come with Olive – I'd take her and he'd stay at home just pottering around in the house or the garden. At the time he was enjoying the campaigning but we could all see that the stress and hassle was having an effect.*
>
> *"Anyway, an assessment appointment was booked for Ron, and I agreed to take him. Olive came with us because she had an injection on the same day. On the way to Bath Ron developed agonising stomach and back pains which were so bad that he could barely sit in the car. I called at a friend's because I thought she might have painkillers that were strong enough to take away the pain while we continued to hospital – it was that bad.*
>
> *"We arrived at the eye clinic and Ron was still in terrible pain. Olive had her injection but we were most worried about Ron because he seemed to be deteriorating rapidly. He got as far as the machine which would be examining his eyes but clearly he was in no condition to go through with the examination. The consultant said that we should get his stomach pains examined as quickly as possible so we took him around to A and E. Obviously there was something very chronically wrong with him and we expected he'd be seen immediately the moment we arrived at A and E.*
>
> *"Sadly, we were wrong. He was kept in A and E for about four hours in complete agony, then he was put on a trolley and*

left there for 24 hours before he was transferred to an assessment ward. It was absolutely outrageous and although I complained and complained no one seemed to be interested in doing anything about it. He was saying, 'I don't think this is right', which was a complete understatement but Ron was a polite man and not one to complain unnecessarily.

"Finally he was transferred to an assessment ward and even there very little seemed to be happening. His breathing deteriorated and we really thought he was going to die. It was the most awful situation."

Finally, Ron was diagnosed with bone cancer which had spread up his spine. He was very, very ill and at this point I knew in my heart of hearts that he wasn't going to make it. My only hope was that he would be made as comfortable as possible. But no. This wasn't to be. I'll let Bella continue:

"He was given some X-rays and quite honestly, they were handed to him as though they were holiday snaps. There was no consideration at all. They appeared to show there was a mass on his lungs which we all assumed was lung cancer. It wasn't. Unfortunately, the appalling conditions he'd been kept under for days on end had led to him contracting C.Difficile, plus a serious chest infection and vomiting and diarrhoea. He was in a terrible state and we thought he would die there and then.

"We asked whether Ron could be put in a private room so we could have somewhere quieter to say our goodbyes but were told this wasn't possible because there was someone more ill than Ron who needed their attention. We'd all arrived at the hospital by this time but as we were trying to have a peaceful time we were constantly interrupted by noise, shouting, nurses asking if Ron wanted soup or tea. It was just shocking.

"Finally we found a side room and practically demanded that

he be moved in there. While this was happening we were told by a doctor that at no time was Ron dying. Well, it didn't look like that to us.

"He was pumped full of morphine which gave him hallucinations. He was talking very strangely, saying there were aeroplanes flying around the bed, and he was sitting up and appearing to be controlling a radio set. It was like he was reliving his wartime experiences. At this point we just wanted him out of there because we couldn't see him recovering, but he couldn't be released into the care of a private nursing home because, of course, he'd contracted one of these hospital diseases. It was a terrible situation."

After a few days the disease he'd contracted seemed to have subsided and it was considered that he could be allowed to go home. I was as pleased as you could be in such horrible circumstances and he was allowed to go home on April 10. The sister who released him into our care advised us to make the best of the time we'd got with him, so I knew then that he was dying. He came home in an ambulance, along with all the special equipment he needed, and he was so pleased to be in familiar surroundings after such a bad experience.

That day we sat him in his favourite chair and although he was on morphine he seemed happy enough. He watched football on the TV with the dogs at his feet. The following day I had to go back to the RUH for my usual injection and while I didn't want to leave him I knew that it had to be done. He woke up that day and he said to me, "I'm very ill, you know…"

"I know you are," I replied. By this stage he had pneumonia and at his age it's very hard to recover from that.

"I've got a hell of a headache," he said. "Do you think I could do with some Vicks?"

I could've laughed. Of all the things! Vicks wasn't going to do much to make him better but he was insistent that he put some in a bowl of hot water and lean over it with a towel covering his head. It's what our generation always did to relieve congestion in the nose and on the chest. It wouldn't do a scrap of good but I wasn't going to say that. So I did this for him and told him I'd be back from Bath at 4pm.

When I arrived home the family was around, along with the doctor. Ron was in bed and it was clear that he wasn't going to last the night. He was given another dose of morphine and within three hours he'd slipped away. Before he died, I held his hand and said, "Well, Ron, we've come a long way since we first met in the parish hall." "Yes, we have," he replied quietly. "No regrets?" I shook my head and smiled. Of course I had no regrets. We'd had a long and amazing marriage, with many adventures. We'd had our ups and downs of course, just like other couples, but we'd had a tremendous life together. My sadness was that he'd had to suffer so much in the last few weeks of his life and that only in the last day was he comfortable. At least he made it home.

I knew how ill he was, but his death was still a tremendous shock for us all. I went to stay with Nigel while the undertaker came and did what he needed to do. His funeral was at Westerleigh Crematorium, near Bath, and we gave him the best send-off we possibly could. A few days after the funeral we wrote a letter to the hospital, complaining about his treatment, but we were disappointed by the reply. There was an apology that the hospital had left him on a trolley for 24 hours and they also said that his care was 'on occasions less than ideal'.

What really upset us, though, was the accusation that as a family we had been aggressive towards staff, which the hospital claimed was noted in Ron's medical records. To me, this was most unfair. Ron and I are not aggressive people and when Nigel checked the notes there was no mention of being aggressive. What I did think was that we were somehow being punished for speaking out to the press, first about the AMD funding issue then about Ron's treatment when he was admitted to hospital. I think the coverage in the press embarrassed them – and quite rightly too. Their letter treated us like we'd been a nuisance, which was annoying and upsetting.

Anyway, none of this would bring Ron back and now I would have to learn how to live without the man I'd been married to for almost 60 years. His time in hospital meant that I'd quickly got used to being alone, so at least I had some warning of what life might be like without him. And as a footnote to this chapter I will let Bella sum up her feelings about Ron, as she was so close to him:

"I loved Ron like he was my own father. In fact, we were often mistaken for father and daughter because he had quite dark skin for an Englishman and I'm of Indian background. My relationship with my own father was complicated and we weren't close, so when I met Nigel, Ron and Olive became sort-of surrogate parents and that's how I've always thought of them both.

"Ron was a smart man in all senses of the word. He dressed well, always in a shirt and tie, and was sharp and clever. He had a great sense of humour and liked his routines. Whatever he was having to eat, the table always had to be set properly, even if it was just muesli! For many years we went to Olive and Ron's for Sunday lunch and without fail he would clear up absolutely everything afterwards. We weren't allowed anywhere near the kitchen. He insisted on doing it all.

"He was an amazing grandfather. He and Olive often babysat for us and we enjoyed taking them away on holiday. The kids would play with his hair, styling it all over the place, and he never batted an eyelid. We liked having them close by and involving them in the things we did. Ron was very interested in

the plans we had for the house we eventually built in Malmesbury, and he would regularly come over to watch the progress. His observations and advice were always welcomed — well, almost always!

"He and Olive were a terrific couple. They were kind, generous and adventurous. They taught me a lot about how to live a good life, and how to treat other people. To sum them up, they were good for each other. And you really can't get better than that."

CHAPTER 20 – JUST MYSELF

When someone close to you for so many years dies, you have two choices – sink or swim. Ron and I had known each other since the Second World War and to lose him was devastating. You hear so often of husbands or wives who die within a few months of their spouse because they cannot find a way to go on. It's easy to see how it happens.

I missed Ron terribly, of course. Bella is right – we were good for each other. We didn't always see eye to eye but generally we got on very well and enjoyed the life we lived. I've no regrets there, and I can never say that I wished I'd travelled more! What I missed – and still miss – about Ron is that we had a shared history. We came from the same place, knew the same people and had a lot in common that way. When someone with that shared sense of place and time dies you really feel the loss. It's like a big part of your own past and upbringing has gone too.

In my case, a trip to China might well have been my life-saver. Before Ron's death we'd been invited out there by Nigel and Bella, who were attending the wedding of one of Nigel's business colleagues. I'd said no, because Ron was so ill, but the trip was fixed for about 10 days after the funeral and I didn't much feel like doing anything, least of all take a long trip to China, but Nigel was very persuasive.

"I think you should come, mum," he said. "It'll be the best thing for you."

Reluctantly I said 'yes' and he was quite right. Being there was a tonic. I've always liked Chinese people and their way of life and it was wonderful to be there, especially at a traditional wedding which is such a spectacle. It brought back happy memories of our time in Hong Kong and Singapore, and just a week out there really helped me to come to terms with what had happened and to look to the future.

When I came home I vowed that I wouldn't just sit around moping and mourning after Ron. None of that would bring him back, and knowing him, he wouldn't want me to be like that anyway. Well, he might have done but I didn't! In a sense, I totally reinvented myself. Whereas we'd previously done almost everything together as a couple, now it was time for me to explore life as a single person. I determined to keep busy, so I joined the local Women's Institute and got involved in all the activities and coffee mornings they organise. I went on a diet, bought new clothes, new furniture. I got a mobile phone and a computer and although I struggled a bit at first with them, I persisted and in time I could use both to the standard that I needed. I learned how to shop online and book things via the internet. I joined Facebook and became a member of various groups, including one for people who'd lived in Hong Kong in the 1960s and 70s. I love being in that group, and hearing everyone's reminiscences of those memorable days.

I took up painting again, despite my sight, and have carried on ever since. I'm very proud of what I seem to be able to achieve, even though I can't always quite see the finished result. People wonder how I do it – I wonder myself sometimes too, but I carry on and I really enjoy it. I wrote too, poetry mainly, and that became a source of pleasure and inspiration for me.

I continued to live alone because I was happy where I was. I wanted control over my life and to feel that I had a good degree of independence. As I've mentioned, for my 80th birthday I returned to Hong Kong with the family on the proceeds of the car I'd had but hadn't driven much. I sold it and we went back to the place we'd all loved. For me, it is a second home.

All that said, I was aware that I wasn't getting any younger and while I loved the bungalow, sometimes it felt that it was all getting a bit too much for me. Our beloved dogs eventually died and the garden suddenly seemed quite big and unmanageable. One day I was out shopping with Bella and her friend in Cirencester and we walked past a McCarthy and Stone retirement complex that was just being built. I stopped and looked at the big advertising billboards they place outside such developments and something about the idea of independent living, but within a secure community, appealed to me.

I mentioned to Bella how good it looked.

"Do you think you'd like to live somewhere like that, mum?" she said.

"Well, I don't know," I replied. "But it certainly looks rather nice, doesn't it? And it would be handy, with you in Malmesbury and Colin in Cheltenham."

Bella seemed very pleased that I'd mentioned it. "I'll have a word with Nigel tonight," she said, "I think he feels you may need to do something about moving."

Nigel rang me the next day. He'd obviously done a bit of research because he suggested we look at a McCarthy and Stone development in Tetbury.

"Over my dead body," I replied. If I'm honest I'd never liked Tetbury much. It seemed to be one of those places you passed through in the car and it was full of antique shops. I like modern things, not other people's objects from the past.

"There's nothing for me in Tetbury, Nigel," I said, "it's just not my scene."

As it turned out, the development was on the edge of town and Nigel had discovered that an apartment inside the development was for sale, with a reduction in the price. So I was persuaded to go and have a look the following day, which we did.

We looked at a couple of apartments but it seemed some negotiation had to take place on the one for sale before we could commit to it. So that happened, and meanwhile I took a real shine to this apartment. It was on the ground floor, so no struggling upstairs or into a lift, it had a garden out the front and nice views on to the road. There was a big garden at the back for everyone to use, plus a communal dining and sitting room if I felt sociable (which I often do!).

"Well," said Nigel, "how about it, mum?"

I must admit that I really liked it and could see myself in there. Nigel suggested putting the bungalow on the market and it took me no time at all to agree to this. The following Monday Nigel called to tell me that Bella had been down to the complex again, a price had been agreed and that they'd bought it.

I was flabbergasted but delighted that I could move in as soon as it was ready. Meanwhile, the bungalow would be sold and the proceeds banked for whatever the grandchildren might need in the future. So that's how I came to be here, in this terrific place with all the lovely people I've met and enjoy socialising with. And no, I don't go into Tetbury! Well, very rarely. The shops are the kind of places you have to make an appointment to go into and they're full of second-hand stuff. That's not my scene. I prefer Malmesbury. The shops are much nicer.

Earlier in the book, I mentioned that I had attended the Queen's 2018 Garden Party. This came about because Nigel decided that the things I had done for the Guides and my work with the Army in Hong Kong were worthy of some sort of acknowledgement. Nigel also pointed out Ron's contribution to the nation, and how I'd supported him throughout, following him all over the world. Unbeknown to me he had written to the Lord-Lieutenant of Gloucestershire singing my praises and making a case for me to be invited.

Well, it happened, and in 2018 I was privileged to be invited to attend a Royal Garden Party at Buckingham Palace. I was invited by the Lord Chamberlain on the 'command' of her majesty the Queen. I was invited for a lifetime's service to the Brownies and Guides in Singapore, Malaya, Hong Kong and Cheltenham, and for my service to the British Army in Hong Kong.

I was accompanied by my beautiful daughter-in-law Bella, Nigel's wife. As a surprise, Bella had booked us into The Ritz for the night. When we arrived at The Ritz things went somewhat awry! There was no one at the door to help us in with our bags, so we struggled up the steps to check in, and when we went to our room we were so disappointed because it stank of smoke and we had specifically requested a non-smoking room. Bella, not being one to put up with anything that was not perfect and having been told by her father-in-law Ron not to accept second best, complained to the management.

While the hotel was sorting this out, we went for lunch; only to be told that the restaurant was fully booked! Bella hit the roof and demanded to see the Manager. While talking to the manager, a very tall, distinguished-looking and smartly-dressed gentlemen approached us and introduced himself as Mr Love, the Chairman of the Ritz. He wanted to know what the problem was. Bella explained in no uncertain terms how disappointed we were with the Ritz, and the problems we had had – and that we were at the hotel as my 90th birthday treat, and not only that, but we were off to Buckingham Palace at 4pm and could not be late!

He said, 'No problem, leave it to me,' and he immediately upgraded us to the best 2-bedroom suite on the top floor overlooking Green Park. He organised for us to have lunch in the restaurant 'on the house' with the best Ritz champagne; he then insisted that they provide a Ritz wheelchair for me to take to Buckingham Palace, saying that I would really need it and that it would get me to the front of the queue at the palace – this turned out to be a fantastic tip!

On arrival at Buckingham Palace, a Coldstream Guardsman in his uniform wheeled me to the front of the queue and into Buckingham Palace gardens. While we waited for the Queen we had our 'tea' - which to be honest was a bit of a disappointment. Two tiny finger sandwiches and a small piece of cake on a tiny plate with a cup of tea, no wine! It was the hottest day of the year with no shade and nowhere to sit; luckily I had my Ritz wheelchair.

Bella always meets someone she knows where ever we go, and the garden party was no exception. She met "Admiral" Paul Mulvaney, a naval officer with gold braid and tassels on his uniform, who was also at the party with his wife Kyla. We always knew Paul as "Admiral" even though his rank was Captain. Paul took over the wheelchair pushed me over the grass to a shady area under some trees where Bella, Paul and Kyla also sat on the grass to 'enjoy' the tea! By this time my cake had melted and gone down the front of my dress and Paul disappeared to get some cloths to clean me up.

Admiral Paul then pushed me to the very front of the crowds to be greeted by the Queen. After two hours in the heat, the Queen eventually came and walked straight past to have her own tea in her own marquee with her own table and chairs. Her tea was a little bit bigger than ours with proper plates, and she had tables and chairs to sit at, and I am sure I saw bottles of wine and champagne being opened and enjoyed by the royal family.

During this period we were entertained by a pigeon who marched up and down in front of us on sentry duty. The Queen then made a quick exit and we decided that we would stay on for a little while to look around the gardens, they were fabulous.

We found a little exit from the gardens and got a taxi back to the Ritz. Mr Love greeted us like long lost friends and wanted to know all about our day. He arranged for an evening meal in the Michelin-starred restaurant and we were joined by my granddaughter Catherine and were provided with a wonderful birthday cake for me.

So after a bad start, The Ritz really pulled out all the stops and made our day unforgettable.

So there we are. My story is now up to date and I hope you've all enjoyed reading it. I've had – and I'm still having - a great life. It wasn't the easiest of starts, but I certainly wasn't the only child in the world who lost its parents at a young age and I was very lucky to have a loving and close family nearby who took me in and looked after me as best they could in difficult circumstances. I regret never being able to treat my 'cousin' Edith as my sister but I'm pleased that I was able to trace my other sister, Eleanor, and have a sisterly relationship with her before she died.

I made a great marriage with Ron and was lucky to have three amazing sons. They're all very different, and very much have their own views about life and the world they occupy. They all had interesting and perhaps somewhat unconventional childhoods, and they've never been afraid to embrace life and pursue their own interests. This approach has meant they've raised their own amazing children – Helen and Andrew to Colin and Sybil; Philip and Megan to Gordon and Lynn over in America; and Catherine, Maiya and Luke to Nigel and Bella. My grandchildren make me very proud indeed, and I love seeing them and hearing how they're progressing through life. There are great-grandchildren too, and I'm sure there will be more of these in the future. I hope I'll be around to see them!

Because I've always been open-minded and ready to embrace new experiences I've met many extraordinary people throughout my life. The military commanders I worked for were very interesting people, and I certainly wouldn't have come into their sphere of influence had I stayed in the North East all my life. General Ronnie McAllister was a particular inspiration. He wasn't just some tarted-up officer straight from Eton. He was no snob – he was the same with everyone he met and a very decent human being who'd fought courageously during the war. Yet his manner was almost professor-like. He was a great person and I enjoyed working for him tremendously.

I think of my grandparents who raised me. I loved my grandfather for his humour and kindness. It can't have been easy for him to accept a small child into his life, especially when there was so little money around at that time, but he did it with good grace and a sense of fun. My grandma was a very tough old lady and there were many times we collided. In the end I couldn't wait to get away and make a life for myself, but again I admire her strength and courage in taking me on.

I also think back to all the young men I knew in East Bolden and Sunderland, the ones who never came back from the war. Even now, almost 80 years on, I feel their loss acutely. They were teenagers, no more than boys, and they went to war with an equal sense of duty and adventure. Ron was among their ranks and, had he suffered the same fate as they did, this story would be very different, or might never have been told at all. Perhaps it was the knowledge of these terrible losses, and what might have been, that spurred Ron and me to travel abroad, embrace different cultures and live a life that was very different to the one pre-destined for us as working-class children from a poor area of the country. We owe that generation a hell of a debt, that's for sure.

I hope that throughout my life I've always been myself in whatever situation I've encountered. I've never put on any airs and graces and I think that's done me good. If you're always trying to be something other than yourself people quickly see through it and you don't get a lot of respect. People like you for who you are, not for what you would like to be if only you weren't you! Being honest and kind in all situations does you no harm at all. I've moved in many different circles and I've always kept my North East accent, which I wouldn't swap for anything in the world. That said, whenever I go home to East Bolden, which isn't often now, and I open my mouth in a local shop or a restaurant, people do ask where I'm from.

"I'm from here!" I say.

"Well, you're very posh," comes the reply. "A posh Geordie!"

And perhaps I am, in a way, though I've never set out to be. All those stepping stones I've taken, ever since I tripped across the ones which spanned the River Wansbeck opposite my first childhood home, have led me to some very interesting destinations. If you're reading this, and you see a stepping stone in front of you, then take it. It might not lead you to where you expect. And believe me, that's a good thing.

EPILOGUE

As I write this, we've just heard from the Government about how they plan to end the lockdown that was necessary to stop the spread of Covid-19. What a year it's been! We've all had to adapt to unusual circumstances and get used to not seeing our loved ones for weeks or even months on end.

Because I lived through the Second World War, people have said to me, "Oh Olive, this must take you back to those times." To which I reply, "Not really." It's a bit similar, in that there was a whole new situation on our doorsteps that we had to get used to very quickly, but the war was in a league of its own. The enemy wasn't an invisible virus, but a whole country that wanted to destroy us. We were bombed from the air every night and our boys had to fight in the most terrible of circumstances.

Even so, I never expected such a pandemic in my lifetime, especially one that affected everybody. We had the AIDS epidemic, of course, and when we were out in Singapore there were a couple of cholera outbreaks which we had to be vaccinated against. I remember my grandmother telling me about the Spanish Flu, which broke out just as the First World War finished. "We were alright," she said, "because we lived in the country.

Only people in the town got it." I don't think that's quite true, but it was the perception among country folk that they were safer. That might be the case today, too.

Anyway, my first experience of this pandemic came when I had my usual groceries delivery. The man from Tesco pressed my buzzer and said, "Your groceries are here but I can't come in." So I went out to meet him and the bags were laid out on the driveway. He was hunched down and he told me he couldn't bring them any nearer. So I went back inside, put my shoes on, and had to carry them all back in, one-by-one. The deliveryman kept apologising and I said, "Don't you worry about me, I'm 92 and blind but I'm fine!"

I told Nigel and Bella about this and Bella said, "We won't let you be humiliated like this again." So I'd send her an email with a shopping list, she'd buy my groceries and pass them through the window. It was a bit difficult at first but we got there. Now there is a trolley at the main door, the deliveryman puts everything in there and we push it down to our rooms.

Although other people in the home have had to get used to shopping online, I've been a fan of it for a while now. It used to be the case that any parcel arriving from Amazon was for me, but not anymore! I love using the internet to shop, and getting regular parcels has kept me going. I never went out from March, when it all started, until June, and although I could sit in the front garden on my own, we weren't allowed to socialise in the back garden or in the communal area. To keep people entertained I'd open my door, put my Alexa out in the corridor and ask her to play songs that I liked, loudly. People used to listen and shout out for requests. I suppose I was the resident DJ for a while!

When things eased up in the summer of 2020 we all got together in the garden, keeping our distance of course. We had a party for Jean, who was 100, and on VE Day we had a sing-song, again in the garden. I did a bit of jitterbugging with Jean, which we probably shouldn't have done, but never mind. A gentleman upstairs with a beautiful tenor voice sang a few songs. It was lovely just to see everyone again.

Then I went into a support bubble with Nigel and Bella and they'd pick me up on a Sunday and drive me over to their house. It was amazing to see the roads so quiet and empty. The best day was when I arrived at their house and Nigel said he had a surprise. He'd bought a golf buggy for Bella as a present, so we got in it and drove down their garden, which is a big one, to the river at the bottom. Well, I got into it and Bella was driving. I was hanging on for dear life because there are no sides to it, but it was fun. On the way back my granddaughter Catherine drove - at a much more sedate pace! We promised ourselves that next time we did this, we'd make a big picnic and have the whole family over for a day by the river. It hasn't happened yet. Hopefully, it will soon.

We also went to London during the summer. I'd always wanted to go to Westminster Abbey and walk in the footsteps of all those who've ever been in there. As a treat, Nigel and Bella paid for me to stay in the RAC Club with Catherine and Maiya, who were lovely and did everything for me. London was so quiet. Only about 80 people at a time were allowed into the Abbey so it felt almost empty. Nigel pushed me around in a wheelchair and it was the most fantastic thing to be able to stand behind the tomb of the Unknown Warrior and look right down the Abbey, and hardly anyone about.

After that, Nigel suggested we go to the Tower of London. It was easy to get a taxi. I had a bit of fun with the man who was giving the talk about the Crown Jewels. Then we went outside and I struck up a conversation with one of the 'Beefeaters' — a lady, as it happened. She was feeding a squirrel, and she told me her accommodation was inside the Tower itself. She'd been in the army before she became a Beefeater and I asked if she was married. "No, I'm not," she replied, "but I've got a canny one now!" Well, we were getting nicely into the conversation when it was time to leave. It was a beautiful day, so we wandered along the river towards Tower Bridge and you could've taken your pick of the park benches to sit on.

To return to domestic matters... I didn't have a cleaner at the time when lockdown arrived. Lockdown meant I couldn't get another one so I thought I could cope, and do it myself. I thought I was doing fine, but when Colin and Sybil came over one day they pointed out marks on the carpet and that the fridge needed cleaning out.

"I can't see any of that," I said, grumpily.

"Well, you won't," Sybil said, "because you're blind!"

"I think it's fine," I replied.

"You've not seen in the corners," Sybil said. "Look, we'll go out now and get a whole lot of cleaning stuff and do it for you."

Which they did, and it was lovely of them to do that. Even if I was still grumpy!

Eventually, I was lucky enough to get my cleaner who used to come when I lived in Milbourne Park. She's called Mel and she's lovely – and from the North East, just like me. She's never lost her accent either. I was so pleased to have her back and I didn't think she'd come all the way from Malmesbury but she did, and she says she doesn't mind. I'm glad she comes because my sight definitely isn't getting any better.

What else did I do during lockdown? I painted a lot. I ordered paints, brushes and canvases online and I just painted and painted. I spent time looking at Van Gogh's work and I noticed how he painted black lines around his flower pictures. So I got some black felt pens and did a few like that. I'm pleased with them and they look even more vibrant when they're in nice new frames.

People have asked if I was lonely. No, I wasn't. Not really. I missed family, of course, but if I felt things were going wrong I'd sit and talk to Ron. Besides, in a place like this you're never completely cut off. People would shout 'Hello Olive!' whenever they passed the door. It was better when we could get out and about, though this winter has been a bit tough. I'd like to walk out more but I can't because I don't see the kerbs very well. My idea of a walk is to go out the front, come round the corner and back in through the garden. Or a stroll around the estate across the road. Bella came recently, though, and we had a nice long walk into Tetbury, then back round past Tesco and home again. That was a long way for me but I did enjoy it.

I have to say that I wasn't frightened of getting Covid. Not when you're 92, anyway. Besides, we're a tough lot, our generation. Maybe it was all that cod liver oil and malt we were brought up on. I'm looking forward to seeing what 2021 brings but I haven't any plans for it so far. I think you'd be a bit daft to make too many plans at the moment. But I do hope we have that family picnic by the river. That'll be something to look forward to.

Olive Roberts, Tetbury, February 2021

Printed in Great Britain
by Amazon

64447241R00163